How to Be a

NOMAD

GO FROM BUSINESS SUIT
TO WORLD BACKPACKER

KIM ORLESKY

authorHOUSE®

AuthorHouse™
1663 Liberty Drive
Bloomington, IN 47403
www.authorhouse.com
Phone: 1 (800) 839-8640

Published by AuthorHouse   02/05/2016

ISBN: 978-1-5049-7144-7 (sc)
ISBN: 978-1-5049-7143-0 (e)

Library of Congress Control Number: 2016901519

Print information available on the last page.

Contents

Prologue

In 2014 I hit my breaking point. I was 31 years old and the day before I ended a relationship with a man that I was very much in love with. For two years he worked out of town and we only saw each other on weekends. Every solution I offered didn't work for him, and I wanted more for us. I didn't know what I was going to do with my life. Every dream I had for us no longer existed.

In the morning I eventually pulled myself out of bed, showered and asked the universe what I was going to do. It sounded so clear in my head, "Go travel."

I pulled the book off my bookshelf that I bought years before, never looked at, yet could never find a way to part with it. It was "The Rough Guide to First-Time Around the World." Today I finally pulled it off my shelf and started reading. I was going to backpack. I was going to leave soon. I was going to do it by myself.

Within 6 weeks of making that decision I listed and sold my house, sold whatever I didn't put in storage, quit my job, and left my dog with my mom. I had never been on my own longer than 5 days when I went on a vacation by myself in my 20s, and now I was going to travel the globe by myself and with a backpack. I didn't even own a backpack. I had to go buy one. The pull that told me that I *needed* to do this was too powerful to deny. I was on a mission and I had no idea where that would lead, but life would provide, and I would have a great story to tell.

Introduction

This book is based solely on my experiences of traveling the world. This is not to be taken as the ultimate guide. The information provided within is based on my personal experience from the time that I was traveling. For specifics or questions that are not provided within this guide please refer to online forums or other resources. I have done my best to be as comprehensive as possible, but information and place change quickly and I cannot guarantee that all information in this book will be completely accurate at time of reading.

Traveling is one of the best experiences I have ever taken in my life. The people I met, the opportunities I was able to experience, all of it was absolutely amazing. It significantly improved the way I viewed the world and life, and I know it will do the same for you too.

Throughout this book I mention several companies that I used for a variety of services. At no time did I receive compensation for mentioning these companies. My personal experience was enhanced by using these companies, and I wanted to mention them to help make your experience just as seamless and enjoyable.

When Is The Right Time To Go

There will never be a "perfect" time to travel. You could spend months or years planning your trip, but for most people I met while traveling the story was close to the same. There was a significant moment in their life that said to them "this is it", and the real planning started. For most people that planning took place over the course of 3-6 months, some others it was several years, and others, such as myself it took place over the course of only a few weeks.

The biggest decision is to actually *decide*. There's no easy solution. Make the commitment that you are going through with it. Decide on the date. Book your first ticket. Then start planning. If you don't take the first significant step there will always be new things that come up: new jobs, new friends, new excuses, new reasons that the timing isn't perfect. Life at home will essentially be the same, however the impact on your entire life that a trip like this has will become less and less the older you get. If you were going to do something amazing for your life, wouldn't you rather do it earlier in your life so you have more time to enjoy it?

To Go Alone or With Someone

This is a decision you have to make on your own. There are advantages and disadvantages to both. In my daydreams I always imagined my trip would be with my future husband, because I was unsure of traveling solo as a female in many of the countries I wanted to visit. However, when I saw my window of opportunity to travel, I didn't have any one to go with, so I decided to go solo.

If you choose to go with someone, make sure you can get along with the person. Extensive travel can take be stressful at times with itineraries and choices such as where to stay, how to get to places, and what to do. An alternative is to have people meet you at different locations or find yourself parting ways from time to time as you both explore your own individual tastes.

If you chose to go alone be cautious and well prepared. You will have the ability to go and do whatever you like. There will be moments of loneliness and a lot of conversations with yourself, but friends can be made easily (and ditched even easier if your company is no longer suiting you). Keep friends and family aware of your whereabouts. Join a tour if you would like company for a week or two. Some of my closest friends now are people I met on short tours.

Costs

This is one of the most difficult questions to answer. I have met people that have traveled solo for 12 months and it cost them $100,000, and others that were able to travel 8 months on $17,000. The amount of money that you plan on spending is completely dependant on the lifestyle you expect to have while traveling, and the number and countries you are planning on visiting. When I left I spoke with one woman that visited several countries in Western Europe and the Mediterranean. For 3 months her and her husband spend about $30,000. I wanted to see many more countries, I was traveling solo, and I knew I did not want to stay in bunkbed hostels. I wanted to say yes to every experience that presented itself. I budgeted for $40,000 and I ended up spending $45,000.

There were several costs that are incorporated before I boarded my first plane. Travel medical services ran into the hundreds. Based on the recommendation of my doctor I updated my tetanus, received a flu vaccination, thankfully I already had my Hep A/B, a double shot for Japanese encephalitis and yellow fever (which proof was required for entry into Tanzania). In addition to the vaccinations I also purchased several prescription medications such as altitude sickness (because I was planning on climbing Kilimanjaro), malaria (which cost hundreds, and I did not even use, deciding to risk the slim chance of contracting it over the side-effects that I heard the pills cause), diarrhea prevention and control, and sleeping pills for adjusting to jet lag.

In addition to the doctor prescribed medications, I loaded my bag up with other over-the-counter medications. I bought everything in pill form for travel ease, and only in small amounts for situations where I could potentially be in a non-English speaking country or a situation where I couldn't get to a pharmacy easily.

See the section Carrying Your Own Pharmacy for items to carry outside of doctor prescriptions.

Other costs that need to be incorporated before taking off include: storage rental fees for your items, pet sitting and veterinary, and return costs while you find new work.

Creating An Approximate Budget

When creating an approximate budget for the country, there are a couple of ways of doing this. You could do a search and find out the approximate cost of traveling through a country, or you could approximate yourself. With a quick search on booking.com, or another accommodation website, find the average cost of a room at a city that you would like to visit within the country. Assuming your budget for the room will dictate how much you would spend in the location, take the room cost, multiplied by two, which would give you your average cost per day. Then use that number and multiply by number of days in that country. This number should cover your standard meals, accommodations, spending money and in-city transportation.

If you are planning on taking a tour, there are plenty of websites that show the costs of different tours. Many tours will include the price of accommodations and half of the meals.

The approximate cost of flights can be calculated by either: 1) getting an around-the-world flight quote, even if you are not planning on book that flight, or 2) the longer version of using a site such as Google Flights or Skyscanner to estimate flights between locations.

Insurance

One of the largest expenses that came out before flying was insurance. This is something that you should not cheap out on. There are two types of insurance that you want to purchase, one is trip cancellation and the other is health. Most credit cards will include trip cancellation insurance, which may or may not include baggage loss or delay. As long as you are booking with your credit card consistently you may be covered without having to take out additional insurance, but it is best to call your credit card company and find out how much of the value and the time limit that this insurance is valid for.

The second type of insurance will require some shopping around: comprehensive health insurance. When booking this insurance it is better to choose a longer time frame than you are originally planning on being away for, in the event you decide to extend your trip. Many insurance companies will refund you the difference of the travel medical insurance upon your return home for the portion that you will not be using. For me, cancellation insurance for the first 30-days of my trip and 9 months of travel medical insurance was about $2000.

Some important questions to ask with travel medical insurance is what types of activities does it cover, what medical services are covered, and how is the insurance applied. Ensure you ask specific questions such as vehicle accidents, as a driver and a passenger. In places such as Thailand driving a scooter can be a dangerous activity, especially when most of the roads aren't paved. Are you planning on going diving, bungee-jumping, or mountain climbing? Think of all the activities you may want to participate in and ensure in the event you are injured during those activities you would be covered. Ensure it is not just basic medical coverage, but comprehensive. Does it cover broken bones, surgeries and exams such as x-rays, and ambulance rides? It is better to pay the additional amount for all of these areas and not have to worry than to be in a situation where, really, anything can happen. The last thing you want is to be on your way to a hospital and having to possibly cut your trip short because one medical emergency that wasn't covered by insurance ended up costing thousands of dollars and therefore cutting your entire trip short.

Visa Costs

Obtaining visas can often be costly. Depending on the country you are obtaining the visa from, this could be as simple as filling out the application and sending in your fee and passport, to a local office, but most of the time couriered to the national embassy of the destination country.

NEVER send your passport via regular mail. Always ensure it is being sent in a courier network with tracking information.

Once you've decided on the countries you are planning on visiting, and have researched what the visa requirements are, plan on purchasing visas for all countries that 1) require visas before arrival, and then optionally 2) visas that can be issued in advanced, if you do not want to wait upon arrival. Visa fees vary by country and by your citizenship. As a Canadian, I have one of the best passports for not needing many visas. The cheapest one was Australia's, which was a $25 fee and purchased online. I only needed to bring the printed receipt. Vietnam was $99 and I needed to send my passport away. India and China took extra work.

The Indian embassy prefers to issue visas within 30 days of arrival, which did not work for me, since it was going to be several months before I was planning on arriving in India. My alternative option would have been to go to an Indian embassy in another country and wait several days for my India visa to be issued. However some visas will have a single entry or a multiple entry visa, for a slightly higher price, which is valid for a longer period of time. I persuaded the woman to issue me a three-month visa valid from 30 days from application, so essentially I was able to take four months before arrival into India.

The Chinese visa also required a multi-entrance visa since I wasn't planning on arriving in China within the next 30 days. Based on their rules they also required my application included proof of flights in and out of the country. I booked a fully refundable return flight, and as soon as I received the visa, cancelled the flight. I lost the cancellation fee, but far better than losing the cost of an entire flight, knowing that I wanted to keep things open to arrival days and departures.

For more information on visa planning, please visit that section.

Travel Budget Checklist

Before Leaving

Realtor or rental management company fees	
Travel medical insurance	
Travel clinic appointment and prescription medications	
Storage unit fees (multiplied by number of months away, and number plus a few extra months to find a new place, if necessary)	
Extra passport photos	
Passport update	
Country visas, including passport courier fees	
Travel purchases, such as unlocking cell phone, new backpack, and clothing	
Pet fees, veterinary and/or resorts	

Travel Costs—By Country, or by average

Flights	
Accommodations	
Meals	
Tours and/or excursions with tips (speak to the tour operator about customary amounts, varies by country)	
Transportation	
Spending money	

Souvenir mailing (average of US$40-$100 every 4-6 weeks, depending on how much you will be purchasing)	
Miscellaneous (10%-15% uplift on the total budget)	

Return Costs

Finding employment (6 weeks to 6 months of your reduced standard of living)	
Memories and keepsakes, such as books and/or framing items	

Deciding on Locations

It can be quite overwhelming deciding on locations and a strategy, but when you start to break it down into smaller pieces, it's not that overwhelming at all.

When starting out make a list of all the places you want to see and all the things you want to do. Do not limit yourself in this process. Give yourself at least a couple of days to make this list.

Once the list is complete enough start to map out the different locations. There are several different online tools that you can use to place multiple pins, or if you prefer, print off a map and pin it manually. Once you see all the locations together you can see if there are any outliers. If there are any specific places that you need to be at a certain time, such as Olympics, World Cup or even Oktoberfest, build that place and time as the centre point and build around from there.

If you do not have a specific destination and date, the next question would be the amount of time you are planning on traveling. Unless you are keeping a completely open agenda, you can approximate spending anywhere from one week (very fast) in each location to over a month. I completed 17 countries in 6 months, which is about a week and a half per country, however some of these countries were commuter countries and not complete destinations. Places such as Kuala Lumpur, Singapore and Dubai were on the way to locations I wanted to spend more time at. Then I would spend two and a half to three weeks at places such as Australia, China, Indonesia and Greece. Because I wanted to cover a lot of ground in limited time I considered the destinations to be the same as multiple vacations.

By this time you should have your mapped out potential destinations with the approximate amount of time you will spend in each place. From this point you will need to start eliminating the outliers. Which locations are too far to get to? Which ones don't fit nicely in the timeframe? You will never be able to do it all.

As you look at the natural progression of locations also consider flights. You may want to avoid any flight that is more than 6 hours, as there may be locations that you could visit in between.

Think about traveling in a generally single direction, ideally west, since that will give you the opportunity to gain time. You can travel north and south within that timezone, but avoid hopping back and forth over timezones as that could be inefficient traveling.

Days Leading Up

What are all the things that need to be taken care of before you can go on the trip of a lifetime?

Thankfully once much of the planning is taken care of, execution is a much more manageable than expected.

Home

If you are lucky enough to be a renter, this is as easy as providing your notice. If you are a home owner you have two options: 1) sell or 2) rent out. There are advantages to both.

In my case I decided to sell my property. The market was at an all-time high. I wasn't completely in love with the house I owned and considered not moving back into it at all. I wasn't even sure if I wanted to settle in the same city. By releasing this additional hold on my life I felt free to explore, plus it was easy to travel knowing I was't going to cause myself any additional debt.

I've also known people that have rented their places. Depending on the length of time, it may be best to hire an agency to take care of the rental for you. For a monthly fee they will be responsible for any issues that arise with the property while you are traveling. They will also source and filter through rental candidates, with you having the final say.

If you are planning on only being gone for a relatively short period of time you may consider renting it out yourself. Ensure you have a back up contact in the event something does occur, such as a plumbing emergency, you will have someone that can make repair arrangements.

Speak with your homeowner insurance, if you are keeping your house, and have rental income insurance placed on the property

The benefits of renting your place out is you will be receiving income while you are away, if only to make the mortgage payments net neutral. You will also know you have a place to come back to, and one less thing to arrange once you are back.

Items and Storage

Whether you are renting or selling your place, the next thing to determine is what to do with your belongings. If you are renting, and a trusting person, you may want to make the transition even easier by renting out your place fully furnished. This allows you to save time and money by not having to pack items away. There will still be a few items, such as certain art, jewelry, clothing, that you would feel better having stored. In this case you may be able to arrange to store them at a friend's place.

If you do decide to pack everything away and use a storage facility, first of all sell everything you do not want anymore. This provides you with a bit of extra spending cash, and it saves you the time of both packing and unpacking an item you really don't want.

If you choose to place everything in a storage unit, try to arrange one that allows you to store your car as well (if you decide to keep it). Car storage can be just as expensive as the storage unit and storage alone can run into the thousands. If you do decide to store your car, speak to your mechanic and find out what needs to occur for car storage. In my case I had a relative go to my unit every 6 weeks and take the car for a drive around the storage facility.

Vehicles and Driving

• Ensure your vehicle's insurance is reduced from driving to fire and theft

• If you don't currently have one, consider getting an international drivers license. I didn't need one, but it would have come in handy when I was in Greece.

Pets

• Have your pet stay arrangements made

• Make a vet checkup and ensure all vaccinations and licenses are up to date and covered for the time you are away

• Update vet records to have an emergency number in place

Cell Phone

• Call cell phone companies and have plans reduced or removed

• Purchase an unlocked phone for easy SIM card replacement, if you decide to go with a phone

Credit Cards

• Call your credit card companies and have notes on your account of the places you are going to prevent your card from being locked while in another country

• Put credit cards on auto payments, if you do not have this already. You will lose track of your days, and your payments, and with auto payments you won't miss any payment deadlines

• If you credit cards use PIN codes, ensure the PIN is four-digits, as many ATMs won't accept more than four-digits

Travel Documents

• Make copies of your personal documents (insurance, passport, drivers license), and email them to yourself. Label the email something unassuming, such as "ticket to ride" or "birthday party details" in the event your email is hacked while in another country

• Ensure your passport has significant time on it, and renew early if needed. Many countries won't admit you if your passport expires within 6 months of arrival.

• Get additional passport photos for applying for visas on arrival

• Apply and receive travel visas for visas that need to be purchased in advance

Other Considerations

• Cancel or place holds on all paid memberships, such as gym memberships

• Purchase and borrow all gear you will need

• Pack your bag a couple days in advance to ensure everything fits and has a proper spot.

Days Leading Up Checklist

More than 6 weeks
- [ ] List house for sale or provide notice for rental property
- [ ] Hire home rental agency, if necessary
- [ ] Secure storage unit, if necessary
- [ ] Place items for sale
- [ ] Apply for new passport, if needed
- [ ] Have extra passport photos taken (5-10)

One Month
- [ ] Visit with travel doctor and update shots
- [ ] Cancel any memberships, cell phone plans, and automatic payments
- [ ] Update vehicle registration and insurance documents
- [ ] Update homeowners insurance with rental property insurance, if necessary
- [ ] Check visa requirements for countries and place applications

Two Weeks
- [ ] Pet vaccinations, vet records and emergency contacts updates
- [ ] Apply and test for international driving license

One Week

- ☐ Contact credit card companies and place travel notes on cards
- ☐ Place credit cards on auto payment
- ☐ Purchase or borrow an unlocked cell phone with replaceable local destination SIM card
- ☐ Ensure all items needed to pack are available and purchased or borrowed

Two Days

- ☐ Pack backpack
- ☐ Create website, fan page or blogging site
- ☐ Make copies of all travel documents and email yourself a copy

Visas

Once you've made the decision of the countries you are visiting check the visa requirements for your passport. Entry and visa fees are based on passport holder, and you should know this before you arrive. The last thing you want is to get to immigration and be immediately denied access into the country because you don't hold a visa for your stay.

Fees, length of time to get the visa, and processes differ from country to country. Requirement on proof for visa also differs. When I was applying for a visa into China I had to prove a flight in and out of the country. For both Vietnam and India I had to mail my passport away. If you are in a time crunch, you need to take these conditions into account.

Check websites to see typical turnaround times for visas and work backwards from longest to shortest turnaround times. In the event you start running out of time for visas, countries that have fast turnaround time can usually also process rush visa services for a slightly additional cost.

1. Determine the list of countries that require a visa

These are the countries that you need to start the application process quickly. There can be delays or additional steps you didn't take into account, and you need to ensure you have enough time to meet all these steps. As well, if you are planning on going from country to country you may have to apply for a multi-entry visa over the single visit to ensure you are covered for the period of time that you plan on traveling.

2. Determine the list of visas on arrival

Many more countries require visas, and you can either purchase them ahead of time or on arrival. If you have time, feel free to apply for these visas in advance. There is no point standing in line if you can apply online in a couple of minutes. Be aware some of these countries may require a minimum time frame for visa purchases to be recorded in their system. Receipts are typically required to be seen as well, and usually electronic versions are sufficient.

If you do decide to purchase visa on arrival ensure you check the cost and the types of currency immigration accepts. Do not assume they will accept their local currency. Depending on the type of county they may ask you for more than the listed visa cost. By knowing what the cost is you won't be paying additional money. It is safe to assume that all immigration lines will accept US$ and many time British Pounds and Euro, but not always the case. They may rarely accept credit card, or there may be an additional fee for credit card transactions. Currency conversions can often times be outdated, so do some quick math and determine what the cheapest currency is.

3. Acquiring visas while traveling

If you are in a situation where you need to acquire a visa while you are away there are several ways of going about it. If you are lucky you may be able to place an order for the visa online. Ensure you have printed off the documents and receipts to prove your purchase. In instances where you need the visa before entering the country you can contact the process of how to acquire one from the country you are currently in. You can have your passport delivered to your home country's embassy to ensure its safe return back to you. However, this process requires that you spend extra time in the country you are currently in.

4. Filling up your passport

In the event you are one of the extreme lucky people to get close to filling up your passport you will need to find your home embassy and have them stitch new pages into your passport. Do this as soon as you think it is close to coming. You may not be close to your local embassy in many of the countries that you are traveling to, and this will require either spending a few days traveling to the city where the embassy is located. Many countries also require a couple of empty pages in your passport before they will stamp approval entry. Ensure you always have a couple of free pages.

Backpack

For the amount of traveling that you will be doing, a backpack is the way to go. Suitcases are cumbersome, even if they have wheels. There will be days where you will have to have your bag with you for hours or overnight trips, and backpacks are easier when you are navigating your way through a big city. Do yourself a favor and invest in a proper bag. Do not cheap out on this purchase.

What you will look for:

• Choose a bag that is no larger than 65L, and even this is the maximum size. I chose a 50L because if I wanted it to join me as a carryon, it would still fit in the overhead bin. Anything larger than this would have to be checked in, or checked below, if traveling by bus.

• The bag should have both a belt strap and a chest strap to keep it close to the body and for best comfort. The belt strap should sit at hip level, and all straps should be fully adjusted.

• Ensure it comes with a rain cover, not just for wet situations, it is also good to place the rain cover over the entire bag when traveling through busy terminals where the potential of having your bag sliced is high. The rain cover acts as a seal where the thieves will have to guess the best place to slice bag, if they do

• Newer bags have the ventilation back, which is what I had, and when you're in humid and hot climates, this is absolutely wonderful

• A removable pouch or section can be useful. If the pouch can be worn as a day bag, then it's useful. Mine had the option to be worn as a belt, which is not, but was useful in the way of keeping items compartmentalized.

• Ensure the zippers have the ability to place locks through them.

• Ensure the straps sit comfortably, and try walking around with the bag when it is fully packed, or put some weight into the bag when trying it out in the store

A good bag will be one of the best things you can invest in. I met many people that invested poorly and they suffered when zippers stopped working, straps broke, or there wasn't enough padding and the straps started to cut into their shoulders.

A great bag will be comfortable and an extension of your body helping you to maneuver through tight environments. Within a couple of weeks you will become a pro at packing it within a matter of minutes, and you may surprise yourself by considering never traveling with anything other than a backpack again.

Clothing

Limited options is the key to this trip. You want to take only absolute essentials, because extra items means doing extra laundry, carrying more weight than you need to, and likely many of the places you will visit will have clothing pieces for incredibly cheap. It is better to buy a clothing item that you need in that moment than to carry around extra items "just in case". And when you do buy something new, it is easier to leave behind an item of clothing that you have worn out than it is to mail it back.

1. T-Shirt

This is your staple item. Choose a color other than black or white. Black gets hot in the sun and white will show stains easily, plus it will never get as clean as you would like it to be when you're washing it in the sink, especially if the tap water is untreated. Choose a color that will compliment your shorts, trousers and skirt. For ladies, if the T-Shirt is longer it can double as a nightshirt for sleeping. Ideally your shirt will be a technical fabric. Stay away from cotton. Cotton dries far too slowly in humid climates, shows sweat, and wrinkle easily. Technical fabrics on the other hand are made for keeping you cool in extreme heat, keeping you warm in cool climates, and are quick dry. Bring 2 but no more than 4 tops. You can mix in a singlet or tank top, but ensure at least 2 of your items have covered shoulders, especially if you are planning on visiting conservative countries or temples where you must have shoulders covered.

2. Breathable, Collapsible Rain Jacket

Find a jackets that is durable enough to handle rain, but can fold into the size of a pocket when no longer needed. The jacket is needed for those days where you are caught in a light daily drizzle or a quick, unexpected downpour, before you are able to find shelter. When the clouds part and the sun comes out again you want to be able to fold the jacket up and put it in your day bag. Don't opt for anything expensive in the event it is stolen. Don't choose a heavy fabric jacket, you already have limited room in your bag and you don't want a jacket that you will only wear a handful of times taking up majority share.

3. Micro-Fleece

Outer wear for cold mornings and chilly days. If it is raining you will wear your breathable rain jacket over top to keep you dry and warm.

4. Rain Poncho

Fold it up. Keep it in your bag. When it is raining heavily this is what you will wear. Large enough that it can also cover your day bag, and optionally your backpack. You may think it looks silly when you buy one, but they are life savers. And when you get to countries where monsoon rains are the norm, everyone is wearing them anyway. I bought mine cheap in Vietnam, although I wish I would have had it sooner.

5. Trousers

Buy a pair that you can easily move and hike in. Do not choose black, as it will show dust and dirt too easily. If you choose a pair of zip-aways choose a stylish design. If you choose a style that looks like a utility cargo pant, you're exposing yourself by looking like a tourist. The trousers should have pockets deep enough for your items, with a zipper or an interior pocket built inside.

Ensure they are wrinkle free and lightweight. I choose one pair of grey zip-aways that were perfect when the day started out cool, then later I could convert them to shorts, or I primarily wore them as shorts. I purchased another pair from an active clothing store that allowed the legs to be rolled up in a boyfriend jean style. They were quick drying and had zippered back pockets with deep front pockets.

6. Shorts

If you decide against a pair of zip-away trousers, bring a pair of walking shorts. They should be a respectable length of at least mid-thigh. Ladies, please, leave the daisy-duke cutoffs at home.

7. Dress

This was my go-to throughout my travels. You can almost never go wrong wearing a dress. It is the perfect thing to wear if you are going out. It is light and breezy for hot days. It is incredibly easy to wear. Choose wrinkle-free dresses. With the longer dresses in style, they are perfect to wear if you are visiting temples (as long as your shoulders are still covered). If you choose a dress that cuts above the knees you can wear a pair of capri-length tights underneath that still covers your knees, which is still acceptable for many places. If you are unsure, bring a sarong with you to wrap around your waist. I had three dresses: a floor length one, one with covered shoulders, and a 5-way dress that could be worn as a skirt or tied in a variety of ways for different styles.

8. Sarong

This becomes your everything. The sarong shouldn't be classified as a clothing item, because it does so much more. You will use it as your beach towel. It will become your blanket on a cold train or a pillow on a bus. You can tie it as a skirt or as a swimsuit coverup dress. Don't worry about buying one before you go, I bought mine in Indonesia for a very cheap price. Any beach location will usually sell them.

9. Swimsuit

You need no more than two. One to wear while the other is drying.

10. Swimsuit Cover

You could use your sarong as a swimsuit cover, but I found I was using my sarong as a beach towel and the last thing I wanted to do was put a sandy, salty piece of cloth against my body. There are some really pretty dresses that are simple and casual. If you put one on over your swimsuit you can easily go to a beach casual restaurant for lunch or walk around the town (for those places where it is appropriate to do so).

11. Socks

Keep your feet warm on cold days or anytime you wear running shoes. If you are planning on doing any overnight hikes, bring two pairs. Go to your local athletic store and pay the extra money for a double layer performance sock. The double layer rubs against itself and not on your heels, preventing you from getting blisters during hikes and runs.

12. Underwear

Leave the cute lacy sets at home. You only need 2-3 sets of technical fabric underwear. They may not be the sexiest things ever, but they dry quickly, and are comfortable while walking all day in hot climates. Technical fabrics may be more expensive, but they will last longer. As for bras, 2-3 are fine. If you are planning on bringing a strapless dress, ensure one of the bras is a proper strapless with replaceable straps. Then choose a stylish low-impact athletic bra, with or without cups, that is quick drying. There is nothing more uncomfortable than being in a hot, humid climate and having to deal with boob sweat.

13. Sports Sandals

DO NOT go cheap on this purchase. Your shoes will see more of the world than most people, and when you are walking for as long as 8+ hours a day, your feet are going to thank you.

Choose a fashionable neutral color that you can pair with your shorts or dress when going out for dinner. Choose something with enough cushion that your feet will feel comfortable all day.

Ensure it has a back strap so that it doesn't easily flip off when you are riding a camel, jumping into a boat or running for a train. You want something that is water resistant because when it's raining heavily, it's smarter to wear the sandals because your feet are going to get soaked no matter how good you are avoiding puddles. I choose a pair of black leather sport sandals first, then after a few months the heel strap broke. I then bought a pair of unique gold Haviana flip flops with a back strap which I still have and wear to this day.

14. Running or Hiking Shoes

A comfortable pair of shoes that you either already run in or if you are buying a new pair purchase them a 1/2 size larger with traction. When you are climbing down hill, or your feet start to swell because of all the walking, the extra half size is going to make a massive difference.

You want them to be breathable. If you choose a running shoe ensure it has great grip as they will double as hiking shoes. If you are debating between one or the other, I like the option of running shoes over hiking shoes because when you are in need of a workout, at least you can go for a run. As a packing tip, stuff your socks and other rarely used items inside the shoes to maximize space and ensure the shoes don't lose shape.

15. Bandana

A great bandana is going to help cover your head, keep the dust out of your face and when soaked in water will keep you cool. I like the special sport and travel ones over the classic cloth triangle. They are made out of a technical fabric and stretch, also doubling as a head band.

16. Hat

Choose a collapsible hat or a technical fabric ball cap. Hopefully you are traveling to a lot of sunny, hot locations, and you are going to want to keep your head cool and the sun out of your eyes. For the most part your hat is going to stay in your bag, so make sure when it collapses it doesn't lose its shape or gain lots of wrinkles. I poorly choose a small beach hat that said it collapsed, but when I would pull it out it had wrinkles in the brim and I found it hard to wear after that since it wouldn't sit on my head properly.

Clothing Checklist

- ☐ T-Shirts 2-4
- ☐ Breathable, collapsible rain jacket
- ☐ Microfleece
- ☐ Rain poncho
- ☐ Trousers 1-2
- ☐ Shorts—Ladies 1, Men 1-2
- ☐ Dress 1-3, include a pair of tights if the dress cuts above the knee
- ☐ Sarong
- ☐ Swimsuit 1-2
- ☐ Optional: Swimsuit cover
- ☐ Performance sock 1-2 pairs
- ☐ Technical fabric underwear 2-4 pairs
- ☐ Ladies: athletic bra 2-3, optional: strapless bra
- ☐ Stylish, neutral color sport sandals with back strap
- ☐ Running or hiking shoes (1/2 size larger)
- ☐ Bandana
- ☐ Hat

Items To Pack

Outside of clothing, there are several essential pack items.

- ☐ Cable ties—keeping items together and emergency situations. I used mine to keep a metal panel tied to a truck when driving through the outback
- ☐ Candles—during power outages
- ☐ Compact umbrella—for the rain and hot, sunny days
- ☐ Copies of insurance, passport, medical records, vaccinations and drivers license
- ☐ Crazy glue—keep in its own ziplock bag
- ☐ Deck of cards—great for long waits and making friends
- ☐ Duct tape—wrap it around the sharpie for space saving
- ☐ Ear plugs—especially if you are planning on staying at shared bed hostels, but good for any noisy city.
- ☐ Elastic bands and/or twist ties
- ☐ Extra camera battery
- ☐ Extra memory discs—although these are easy to purchase in other countries, and are sometimes a fraction of the cost
- ☐ Extra passport photos—to make purchasing the visa on arrival much faster
- ☐ Eye mask—my personal favorite thing I brought. If it's dark enough I can sleep anywhere
- ☐ Hair elastics
- ☐ Headband

- ☐ Head lamp—better than a flashlight because you will be able to search your bag easily
- ☐ Laundry detergent—powder, preferably in individual packs. Place in a large ziplock bag in the event of punctures
- ☐ Light weight bike chain (and lock if not all together)—for locking your bag close to you while you sleep, especially in certain hostels and sleeper trains, or anywhere else you may leave your bag out of your sight.
- ☐ Lighter—ensure they are easily accessible to remove from the bag. Flights in china, even if the bag is checked, will require removal of them
- ☐ Luggage Locks
- ☐ Multi-country outlet adapter
- ☐ Multi prong plug in—one of the most useful things you will bring. Too often there is only one available outlet, and of course you have more than one item that needs recharging. Plus having an extra outlet or two can help you make new friends
- ☐ Reusable fork, knife and spoon—eating out can get pricey. Having your own utensils allows you to buy food from markets and grocery stores and save significantly
- ☐ Rope—to use as a laundry line. You don't need more than 10-12 ft (3-3.5m)

☐ Safety pins

☐ Scissors—a small pair for cutting packaging, cable ties and bandages

☐ Sewing kit—a small one with a few threads, buttons and needle.

☐ Sharpie—for writing signs

☐ Silk sleeping bag liner—it needs to be 100% silk, and not a blend. Bed bugs cannot get through silk. They are pricey to buy locally, but you can have one made for far cheaper in countries such as Thailand, Vietnam and Cambodia.

☐ Sink stopper—a large rubber one to cover a variety of drain sizes for when doing sink laundry

☐ Travel soap dishes—not just for soap. Also for keeping small items together and easy to find

☐ Travel towel—dries faster than a regular towel and stays compact

☐ Tweezers

☐ USB outlet plugs—most devices are USB-based and when you use your multi-prong plug-in, you can offer a USB plug for each of your open spots to others

☐ Water bottle—a platypus or other collapsible one is best

☐ Water purification tablets

Carrying Your Own Pharmacy

Although you can usually buy all of these items overseas, I still recommend buying a few emergency items to carry with you. If you are in a dire situation, far from a pharmacy, you'll be happy to have a few items to get you through. In the event you do find a pharmacy, it is common that the person's English level is basic and you will need to describe your symptoms in hand gestures. Thankfully in some of the poorer Asian countries they will sell you only the amount of medicine you need, but that does mean open boxes and you will not have access to the ingredients list or instructions.

Medical care:

☐ Anti-diarrhoea tablets

☐ Antihistamines—even if you aren't allergic, you will be exposing yourself to several new ingredients and elements

☐ Bandages, including self-adhesive wrap and cotton pads in the event of a severe wound

☐ Blister care—I was a fan of the blister balms

☐ Blood type, if you can't remember, in the event you need a transfusion

☐ Bismuth (such as Pepto-Bismol)

- [ ] Cold/Flu
- [ ] Condoms (if needed)
- [ ] Charcoal pills—in the event of food poisoning
- [ ] Electrolyte tablets or powder
- [ ] Eye glasses prescription (if applicable)—in the event you need new glasses
- [ ] Face mask—considered incredibly rude if you are not wearing one while you are sick, but also handy if you are around sick people, dusty conditions, or terrible smells
- [ ] Hand sanitizer
- [ ] Hydrocortisone cream
- [ ] Ibuprofen (such as Advil)
- [ ] Iodine wipes
- [ ] Laxatives
- [ ] Motion sickness tablets
- [ ] Muscle and joint pain medication
- [ ] Thermometer—digital with celsius reading
- [ ] Tiger balm
- [ ] Topical antibiotic cream (such as Polysporin)

Toiletries:

- [ ] Aloe vera
- [ ] Body lotion
- [ ] Bug spray with DEET
- [ ] Contact lens solution (if needed)

- ☐ Dental Floss
- ☐ Deodorant
- ☐ Hair brush or comb
- ☐ Lip balm
- ☐ Pumice stone or a foot file
- ☐ Razor
- ☐ Shampoo and Conditioner
- ☐ Soap
- ☐ Sunscreen
- ☐ Tissues—in many Asian countries it is expected you provide your own toilet paper
- ☐ Toothbrush
- ☐ Toothpaste
- ☐ Wet wipes

How To Pack

When traveling the world it is essential to pack as light as possible. There will be many times when you will walk around for hours with your backpack on. If you are planning on keeping your bag with you as carry-on, you will be limited to approximately 18kg (40lb), depending on the airline. However if you choose to check your bag in, as I did, there isn't much more weight allowance. Most airlines restrict a checked back to 23kg (50lbs), which is already a lot of weight to carry. This means everything in your bag must have a very specific purpose. There is no room for error.

Heaviest items should always go on the bottom of your bag. It will keep the bag upright when it is placed down. Hiking shoes or running shoes go on the bottom. They have a flat bottom to help set the foundation for the rest of the bag.

Inside the shoes place socks, laundry detergent (in a secured zip-locked bag), rope for laundry hanging, and a rubber sink stopper (which can be placed in the same bag as laundry detergent).

Some people will place their power cords in the shoes, but I found that I needed my power cords at daily, sometimes more often, and to have them at the bottom of the bag would be a massive hassle.

Packing cubes are the world's best thing! I have several cubes. Two dedicated to clothes, underwear, sarong, and swim suits. Clothes are to be rolled, not folded. This prevents many wrinkles, in the event you have purchased any items that are not wrinkle-free. It also gives you the opportunity to see more clothing items, and saves valuable space, as rolling compresses clothing more.

One packing cube was dedicated to bathroom items, such as shampoo, conditioner, antiperspirant, toothpaste, toothbrush, comb, soap, body lotion, and facial sunscreen. All liquids were wrapped in their own bag in the event of a leak or rupture. By keeping all the bathroom items together, in the event I was in a situation where I was sharing a bathroom I could pull out the bathroom bag and carry it with me. In the event I wasn't sharing a bathroom, it kept everything nicely together.

I had a couple of other smaller travel bags for items I used rarely, but were always handy, and a waterproof carry bag that I kept my dirty laundry in. Because it was waterproof it prevented making the rest of the bag smell bad, plus it was easy to grab and take to the laundromat or send away for laundry. The waterproof bag was also great for taking to the beach, and it contained my personal items if I was day-tripping while it was raining.

The top of my larger backpack had a removable pouch. Inside the removal pouch I kept all my chargers, outlet adapters, paper souvenirs, or other trinkets, and backpack rain cover (which actually had a dedicated pocket). I also carried an extra book or two. I did carry a kindle, and had to buy a second one, because they were both destroyed during my travels.

Packing and Carrying Your Day Bag

Your day bag needs to be small enough that it can sit comfortably on the front of your body when your backpack is on and large enough to carry one or two nights of items. I chose a small one should sling bag and it was too small for my needs. Had it been slightly bigger it would have been the perfect size.

More often than not your day bag will sit on the front of your body. You should have a few easy to access pockets or compartments where your passport and wallet will be carried. It should have an easy to access external pocket where you will carry your dummy wallet (see the section on dummy wallet).

Don't choose too big of a day bag, because you will typically be wearing it during your daily sightseeing. An alternative for ladies is to also pack a foldable cloth satchel for carrying daily items and leave the day bag for travelling days or overnight excursions. If you chose a cloth satchel, ensure the strap is long enough that it can be worn across the body, as opposed to a single shoulder, and always wear it in the front of your body, and never on the side or behind you. This will prevent many pick pockets.

On a typical travel day your day bag will contain your essentials and valuables. If your backpack wasn't to arrive at your destination, you need to have enough to get you through until you can purchase new items.

Packing Your Day Bag
When Traveling

- [ ] Passport—packed inside the bag, in a zippered pocket
- [ ] Wallet—packed inside the bag, in a zippered pocket
- [ ] Dummy wallet—packed in an external pocket, that is reach to reach
- [ ] Electronics
- [ ] Chargers
- [ ] Medical records
- [ ] Sarong—when traveling overnight, to use as a blanket or pillow
- [ ] Eye mask
- [ ] Ear plugs
- [ ] Toothbrush
- [ ] Toothpaste
- [ ] Water bottle—empty if flying
- [ ] Hair brush
- [ ] Hair elastic
- [ ] Wet wipes
- [ ] Tissues
- [ ] Change of shirt and underwear
- [ ] Book
- [ ] Deck of Cards

- ☐ Pen
- ☐ Paper or notebook
- ☐ Bandana—if you are planning on taking a tuk-tuk or rickshaw
- ☐ Sunglasses
- ☐ Next destination travel itinerary
- ☐ Anything else that you cannot afford to lose
- ☐ Chain and lock—if you are traveling overnight or long periods and will not be sleeping with your bag

Apps and Downloads

• **AirBnB**—a fantastic option if you are going to be any place during high season. Also great for the opportunity to share an accommodation with a local and learn even more about the culture and interesting thing about the area.

• **Booking.com**—There are plenty of accommodation booking sites, including Agoda, Expedia and Hostel Bookers, however I found Booking.com to have the largest worldwide selection, the prices were at least comparable, if not the cheapest, and it includes a wide variety of accommodations, including hostels.

• **Bravolol**—There are many language apps available but this was my preference. Free basic language app, includes speaking. Upgrade by language for even more phrases.

• **Currency converter**—have an idea of the exchange rates before you arrive, then you will know if you are receiving a decent deal. Best if it works offline to help you do quick math when negotiating

• **Dropbox and Carousel** (Carousel specifically for photos)—auto backup all your photos when they are downloaded. Set it so that the moment you hit WiFi photos are being saved and backed up from your phone, or any downloaded photos from your iPad

• **Google Maps**—Works even when you're offline. Star your destination (or origin, in the case of a hotel), and it will use GPS (without data) to show you where you are. You can only get directions when you have WiFi or mobile. Google is also great for transit and will include the buses, trains and subways to take, the time they will be available and the price

• **Scribd**—Monthly Subscription. If you are a fast reader or like to have a variety of books available, this is an amazing app. You have unlimited access to their wide selection of books for a monthly fee. I purchased it for the Lonely Planet guides originally. There were plenty of books to choose from, and since their launch they now include audiobooks.

• **Skype**—Stay in touch for free with friends and family when you have access to WiFi.

Purchase credits in the event you need to make an international phone call.

• **Skyscanner**—Besides Google Flights, which didn't have an app last time I checked, this was the cheapest for booking flights. It is not a booking tool, but rather a flight cost scanning tool.

Flights are then booked directly with the airline. It also provides flexibility for airports and destinations, such as the country instead of the specific city, or any direct flights leaving the current country.

• **TravelPod**—My preferred travel blog. Includes picture upload, map of locations, auto post to Facebook and Twitter, and the ability to print your entire trip into a hard cover book

• **Triposo**—Travel Guides for countries and cities around the world. Select the sites you would like to see and it will create a walking tour for you to navigate. Also includes handy local phrases and traveler comments about hotels, tourist traps and things to do

• **World Lens**—Paid. Recently bought by Google Translate and is limited in language capabilities, but will translate certain languages live and offline. Just looking at this app it's pretty amazing

• **World Trip**—Paid and optional. I used this app as my currency converter and to keep track of all my flights and accommodation reservations. It will keep track of flight cancellations and delays and send notifications. It was also handy for keeping track of the multiple time zones.

Booking Flights

If you are choosing to be fully prepared and planned for your trip a world-ticket may be a good option for you. This can be purchased through World Alliance, or one of the other group airline sites. There are certain restrictions on the tickets. You can only travel in one direction and all flights need to be booked at time of purchase. However you may want to look into some of the restrictions. Sometimes if you book a world flight, and there was a need to cancel or delay a flight, you are still paying for a cancellation fee. It may also be if you cancel one leg, the entire package is cancelled and you have to rebook everything again. For me, I found this to be too restricting. I ended up buying one-way tickets throughout the entire process.

There are a few different flight sites that offer great flight results. I primarily used Skyscanner as it provided options into surrounding airports. There are no fees since it sources ticket prices and purchases are made directly with the airline. You can set price notifications to let you know if the price has changed. If you are feeling completely open you can set the origin destination and ask it to find you the cheapest flight anywhere.

If you are planning on going to a new destination and will likely have to layover (or if you are looking for a layover) I was informed by other travelers that Kayak was a great way to purchase these flights. They offer 48 hours of layovers with no additional cost. Cities such as Singapore, Kuala Lumpar, Dubai, Tokyo, Los Angeles and Hong Kong are usually the most common layover cities, and often times 48 hours is just enough to see the highlights. Singapore even offers several sightseeing tours from anywhere of a couple hours up to 8 hours, leaving and returning to the airport. Although you don't really need to leave, as it is the coolest airport in the world.

If you like staying flexible I found as long as flights were booked at least 4 days in advance, and better if up to 2 weeks, you were able to capture the cheapest deals.

In many of the Asian countries, such as Thailand, China, Indonesia and Vietnam flights were incredibly cheap. With your time, I recommend never opting for a bus or train if you can save yourself hours by taking a flight. Use your time for enjoying beaches and markets, not commutes. However, ensure you are experiencing a variety of transportation types, with flights you miss out on the landscape and meeting new people.

Jetlag

Jet lag can be a terrible thing if it is not prevented even before the flight. The best way to get over jet lag is to sleep as much as possible on the plane. This could seem like a terrible task for people that have a hard time sleeping on planes, but it is absolutely necessary if you are wanting to be functional during the hours that the destination location is awake. The best way to do this is to sleep as soon as you can when you are on the plane.

When you book your flight indicate you have a dietary restriction. This will ensure you are fed before all the other guests. Once you are finished your meal, or even right before you start take a sleeping pill. Prescription pills are better than over-the-counter as they are created to help people fall asleep quickly for short-term bursts without feeling groggy. My personal favorite was Zopiclone. A half a pill was enough to help me fall asleep right away. When speaking to your doctor before traveling let him or her know you are taking long-distance flights and they should have no problem prescribing a small amount of sleeping pills. Over-the-counter pills can be effective, but I found if I woke up in the middle of a sleep, and had to take a second dose I felt groggy during the day.

Prepare as well as you can for a comfortable sleep. This includes your eye mask, ear plugs, sarong in case you get cold, or you can roll it up into a pillow.

Sleep as much as you can. Over sleep if you can. When you do wake up periodically ensure you are walking around, stretching, do a few squats by the bathrooms, and drink plenty of fluids. Water and electrolytes will keep your body nourished.

When you land hopefully you will be so well rested you will not be able to fall asleep an-ytime soon. Spend the first couple of days avoiding sleeping too early or late, and the same for waking up. Put yourself on the local meal schedule immediately, whether you are hungry or not. By eating at regular intervals you will give your body the energy it needs and will likely push off fatigue for a few hours more. Finally, be active. Walk as much as possible. See the sights, and just keep moving.

Transportation

Once you leave the comfort of your own country, it's amazing all the different forms of transportation that are available. I highly encourage you to do your best to try the many different kinds, however it is a very fine balance between experience, price, and time.

Flights

Flying is absolutely the best way to get around. If you can take a flight, do it. Especially in may Asian countries, such as China, Vietnam, and Indonesia, flights are often as cheap as any other form of transportation. Flights are easy to book. Regional flights can easily be booked by walking into any travel agency, plus you may be lucky enough to have the travel agent invite you to their place for dinner. If you are really last minute, head to the airport and book a flight from the ticket counter. Just ensure you are there with plenty of time so you can navigate to your gate and go through security, since security rules differ country to country.

If you are planning on flying more than 6 hours, do your best to book an overnight flight. Save yourself the cost of a hotel by sleeping on the plane, if you are able to sleep on planes. Be prepared the morning can often be long as you have to usually stay awake for as long as you can until your room is available by mid-afternoon.

Ferries

Ferries are common for both domestic transport and international. If you are prone to sea- sickness ensure you take a sea-sickness pill shortly after entering the ferry to give it enough time to set in. Ferries are also easy to book at any terminal or travel agency. They will often provide you with the time that the ferries leave the port, but you have to ask if it is a direct or a multi-stop, and the expected time of final arrival. I made this mistake and ended up being on a ferry for 6 hours, and 3 stops, from Lombok to Bali, where the flight would have cost the same price and I would have arrived 4 hours earlier.

Ferries in the Middle East work differently, as the times of departure are completely up to the crew. You will likely get an approximate time of arrival, but the departure time could be hours later. Have yourself prepared to spend hours on the ferry. Pack snacks, things to do, and items for napping.

There are usually two types of ferries, a standard and the high speed. Depending on the time you have, it may be best to opt for the additional price on the high speed ferry.

For ferries that have booked seats, they will typically offer a standard and a first class fare. I found this to be the case in Greece, and when I did book the first class fare, which I did for an overnight ferry, it wasn't worth the additional price. There was a little bit of extra room, but in terms of what I would have expected from first class, such as reclining seats, it did not offer that. If booking with an agency clarify what the cost and quality difference is between the classes.

Whatever you do, avoid booking an overnight ferry. This is especially the case if you are already prone to sea-sickness. You will not get any sleep during this time. But more importantly, it's not just for you, but depending on the size of the ferry, there will be at least a couple of people that are prone to sea sickness and anything more than a few hours on a ferry is going to do them in.

As a passenger, a ferry with a few sea-sick people on it is a very uncomfortable experience. If you do choose an overnight, ensure you have your sarong (or a blanket), eye mask, and earplugs for a restful sleep. It may even be in your best interest to ensure you bring a face mask with you, to hold back the smell of people getting sick.

Ferries for international transportation are one of the easiest ways to cross the border. I used a ferry for both Turkey to Greece, and again from Egypt to Jordan. Typically the passport line ups aren't too bad, and in some of the poorer countries, look for a tour group going at the same time. It's worthwhile to ask if you can tag along, since they usually give tourists better service, and you may be able to enter the ferry sooner.

Keep an eye open for your bag at all times. It's not the same as checking it in at an airport. They are typically all thrown together and dumped out in one large mass at the end of the ride.

Always push and see if you can keep your bag with you. There are no guarantees, but if you don't ask the answer will always be no. Worst case scenario ask if there is a lock up area that your bag can be placed. But in this case it is always best to have an unassuming bag that does not look touristy.

Bus

There will be the standard bus and then there are sleeper buses: bunkbeds on a bus. Buses are the most common way of getting around many countries. As said before, if there is a plane option, always take the plane. However buses in Turkey are amazing, include cart service, and typically ice cream.

For longer rides the bus will usually stop every two hours or so. Plan your drink and food intake accordingly. Many buses don't have toilet facilities, plus if they did you likely don't want to be using them. Never leave the bus without taking a picture of the bus number, or at minimum jotting down the number. Many buses look the same and you do not want to get on the wrong one or miss yours completely. It also helps to meet someone else on the bus, or the driver, so they keep an eye out for you.

The sleeper buses in China usually are a maximum length of 5'5" (165cm), so if you are taller than this, it can be an incredibly uncomfortable experience. It is not uncommon to see the occasional person taller than 6' (182cm) sleeping on the floor of the bus.

The sleeper buses do include sheets and blankets for a comfortable night. Remember to keep your valuables in your day bag, which you will sleep with, and have your eye mask and ear plugs with you.

If there is any reason you will exit the bus without your day bag, ensure you lock it up, and to something permanent. There are stories of people running onto buses and stealing bags, and if yours if locked up, you can feel safe that yours may be left behind by the running thieves.

Train

Trains are a great alternative in the event you can't find a flight, or you are in a country with high-speed options. Trains are one of the primary sources of transportation in Japan, and the country is surrounded in the high-speed variety.

In Japan train tickets are assigned by car and seat number. Ask anyone to help you to ensure you are on the right area of the platform for the arriving train. You can still walk the length of the train to get to the correct car, but it becomes harder when you are navigating you backpack around cart service.

There are also two types of trains, multi-stop and express. Always ensure you are taking the most direct route there, otherwise your trip will take longer than necessary. The trains also connect to the subway and metro systems, so you do not have to take any other form of transportation once you are there. There is service on the train, but you are allowed to bring your own food, and beverages, including alcohol, on the high speed trains.

In some of the poorer countries, such as India, purchase the first class fare, especially if riding for overnight travel. The lower classes are typically filled with standing people, and as a tourist you are at risk of being robbed very easily. Pick pockets are all over. With a higher class fare you are also given access to an air conditioned room while waiting for the train to arrive, which in some cases delays can be into the hours.

Depending on the country, first class will usually include a meal (or two for overnight), however you will still benefit by brining your own snacks and beverages since some of the delays between stations can be long. Ensure you have your eye mask, ear plugs and a deck of cards.

If you are on a sleeper train that is not in a cube, ensure you use your bike lock and chain to lock your bag directly underneath you. Always sleep with your valuables. Someone can still cut your bag away from the bike chain, but at least you will still have your passport, electronics and credit cards with you.

Many train tickets need only be purchased the day of travel, but it can be helpful if you purchase them a day or two in advance.

For non-English speaking countries if you have a calendar and a picture of the next destination, or a map, that can help you to purchase the right ticket.

Taxis

Taxis exist in every country, although what that means is up for definition. In countries such as Indonesia it is not uncommon to see men holding signs that say taxi, and after negotiating place and price they will bring around their own vehicle.

When arriving from the airport there are two options for taxis, choosing a metered fare or a flat rate. I typically always went with the flat rate. I knew what I was paying and it was never in the interest of the taxi driver to drive longer than he (or she) absolutely had to, which was perfect with me since I often wanted to have my bag dumped as soon as possible at the hotel.

You will always have two choices when taking a taxi, going with the metered fare or negotiating *before* you enter the vehicle. If you choose to go with the metered fare, have your google map or GPS set so that you know where you are going, and be confident enough to challenge the driver if the route is off course and your fare is being raked up. If you choose to negotiate ahead of time, have an idea of the fare, or start by asking the driver what he (or she) would charge, then negotiate from there. If the driver will not negotiate beyond a price which seems unreasonable, walk to the next cab. Someone will drive you for the price you set.

If you are traveling with your backpack, do your best to travel with it in the back seat with you. If you must put it in the trunk of the vehicle, do not exit the vehicle before the driver. Or if the driver has opened the trunk, do not close your car door until after you remove your bag. This is a preventative measure so the driver does not leave with your bag still in the vehicle.

In some of the wealthier cities, such as Kalua Lumpar, there is WiFi in the vehicles. A great bonus to ensure your maps, airline tickets and hotel bookings are loaded on your phone or iPad.

Shared Taxis and Mutatus

This is an experience in itself! Shared taxis and mutatus (as they are called in Kenya and Tanzania) are about the size of a full-sized van, and filled much more than you would expect one to be. Luggage is usually stored on a roof rack and covered with a tarp, so it is usually a good idea to put your rain cover over you bag before handing your backpack over. This will prevent any wetness, but more likely extra dust from entering into your backpack.

When buying a ticket there will be a pickup location and a pickup time, which can really be up to the driver. Seats are sometimes assigned, and it is worth asking the person selling you the ticket where you are sitting. Ideally you want to be in the second row, as that is the safest place to be in the event of a car crash. However in hot climates you may be better asking for the front seat, closest to the air conditioning. Also ask if you are getting a single seat or a shared seat. You may have to pay for two tickets because if you pay for a shared seat expect to have someone sitting on your lap, or you sitting on someone else's lap. Literally. All that said, it is an experience like no other. Make sure you have music or a good book, the ride can be long.

Public Transportation

Public transportation is one of the best ways to get around and immerse yourself in a local culture. I found the individuals to be incredibly accommodating with people always wanting to help.

It can become a bit nerve-racking taking a bus to a destination, as they will almost always be in the local language, whereas a train or subway will usually have some English translation, even if it is poor. Feel free to ask the locals what the correct bus to enter is, sit as close to the driver as possible, and ensure he knows where you would like to get off.

Google Maps does an amazing job with helping to take transit now. It will show you walking directions to the bus stop, show you the number of stops, and transfers, if necessary. It will usually also include the cost of the trip.

In some countries there may be "women only" cars for the trains. This is a wonderful experience for females traveling solo. They are feel a bit safer and it is more respectful for women to talk amongst themselves. If you are a couple, you can travel together in the mixed car, or feel free to split up and meet up again on the platform.

Tuk-Tuks, Rickshaws, Motorcycle Taxis

You will see these different forms in most Asian countries. Tuk-tuks look slightly different in many countries, but they will be a covered transport that is on its own or pulled by a motorcycle.

They are fairly safe, do not travel very fast, and can fit two people comfortably, or two people with baggage or three squeezed in.

Rickshaws are pulled by a bicycle and although they cannot go significant distances, they are a great option for tired feet, or to see cultural neighbourhoods.

Motorcycle taxis are exactly that. A motorcyclist, or scooter, will have room for one person. You may be able to take your bag, either by wearing it, or the driver may put it up front with him.

There are no helmets, so take caution. Keep your body tight to the driver, and either hold onto the bar behind your seat or onto the driver. Move with him and lean into turns, not away.

Depending on where you are, these are great options to move in traffic, but hold your body close. They will swerve in between cars, pedestrians and buildings.

All three are great options for hiring for the day if you have plenty of sightseeing to do. ALWAYS negotiate with the driver before entering the vehicle. In one case I took a rickshaw in China about 12 blocks. Out of exhaustion I didn't negotiate before entering and the driver charged me US$60, the same cost as my flight from Beijing to Xian. I was absolutely irate, and there was little I could do about it after the fact.

Because these modes of transportation are completely open, make sure you have your bandana and sunglasses with you. The roads can be dusty and it can be difficult to see and breathe with the amount of dust flying in the air.

Flatbed Trucks

This is a very regional option, but still widely used in parts of Asia and the Middle East. Typically it's a flat bad truck, with a cover and a couple of bench seats in the flat bed. The truck stops when you wave it down. It's usually a flat fee to take you where you need to go, but it does travel on a general route. If there are no other people waiting in the back, feel free to negotiate, but make the negotiation fast, as in find out the price and then tell the driver what you will pay, and have that money ready.

Be careful with these trucks. There are no seat belts. People will be jammed in until there is standing room only. Finally you need to be aware of where you need to get off. Sometimes there is a bell that lets the driver know you want to stop. More often it's about banging the side until the driver stops, or taking advantage of a stop in progress.

Boats

For many island nations boats will be the typical way you can travel. You can hire a private boat or a group boat in the event there isn't a ferry. Always opt for the speedboat if you are given an option. There will likely not be any life jackets. Put your rain cover over your bag to prevent splash, and prepared to get wet. Once the drivers know what they are being paid they will try to get you to your destination as quickly as possible, even to the point it is slightly ridiculous how fast they are driving.

Donkeys, Horses, Elephants and Camels

This isn't really your standard transportation to get you from point A to point B, but they are so fun I have to mention. Every country has their own preference to animal. They will typically be used for tourist attractions. In the case of Santorini, Greece, donkeys are used to help walk tourists up the many stairs from the port to the boardwalk.

Please use discretion if you decide to hire one of these animal handlers. Many of the animals are treated fairly well, and many others are not. The good handlers know these animals are more like pets, they are cared for, and loved, because if it wasn't for the animal they would lose their primary source of income. Before hiring an animal check to see if the animal is kept in shade while waiting. Does the animal look healthy? Do they have access to water? What kind of tool is the handler using to guide the animal? Is it a rope or is it a prod? If you don't feel good about the relationship between the handler and their animal it is best to let it go. There will be lots of opportunities to ride these animals, maybe even as close as a block away. Please do your best to make ethical choices and ensure your money is going to those who enhance the lives of others.

Thankfully there are simple ways you can research and find out what are proper people and companies to deal with. This isn't just advice for transport animals, this is also great advice for paying to see elephant and tiger "orphanages". Please do your research and ensure the animals are treated how you would your own pet.

Negotiating for Transport

Almost everything on your trip can be negotiated, transportation is one of the biggest ones. Be reasonable when negotiating. Many of the locals use their services as the only source of income for their entire family. However always know what you will be paying

BEFORE entering the vehicle. If you chose to enter the vehicle and go off a meter, ensure you already have your destination mapped out so that driver does not take you on a very expensive tour of the city, which happened to me in Ho Chi Minh City.

Some drivers will agree to a price and then partway through will try to negotiate additional payment, let the driver know you are fine to exit the vehicle right there, and be bold enough to do so. In India a rickshaw driver agreed to a price and then as we drove he kept saying a higher price. Hold your ground. I told him to take me only to the place I wanted to for the amount we agreed. I did not need additional sightseeing or services.

Most importantly have fun and experience as many different modes as you can. It is part of the local experience.

Accommodations

In Japan I was talking with an older woman who was also traveling the world. We talked about booking accommodations. She would spend hours looking at different hotels on different travel websites and reading various reviews. I felt horrified for her. She was spending more time thinking about her next hotel and not enough time enjoying the places that she was currently in.

I told her when I first started traveling I spent a lot of time comparing hotels but eventually simplified my process. I selected hotels based on location and filtered out based on amenities and traveler score. I spent far less time booking hotels, and for the most part they were just as good as what I was needing. The moral of the story, don't over complicate this process. There will always be a cheaper or better accommodation; focus your time on enjoying and not planning.

I used Booking.com for all my accommodations. There are plenty of booking sites, such as Agoda and Expedia, and ones dedicated to hostels, however, I found Booking.com had the best selection of accommodations worldwide for the same price. Booking offers hostel accommodations, and the ability to filter by map and amenities.

As I traveled I learned the best thing to do was book only one or two nights (if I was only planning on staying in a place for two nights) and then check out the neighbourhood. If I liked the accommodation, I would ask the front desk for additional nights, sometimes, but not always, offered at a reduced cost. If I showed up and it wasn't what I was expecting, then I only had to stay there for one night and I could find another accommodation either through Booking.com again or by walking into any other hotel/motel/hostel and asking in person what they had available.

Questions To Ask

• **Is WiFi included or an additional cost?** This could make your "cheap" accommodation not as great of a deal if there is an additional $25 fee for WiFi (and yes, this is sometimes the case).

• **Is WiFi in the rooms, or only in common area?** This was important for me when I would be making late night or early morning Skype or FaceTime calls back home. This is also essential when loading pictures to Dropbox or TravelPod overnight.

• **Shared bathroom or individual bathroom.** Typically only necessary if you are planning on staying at a hostel.

• **Is there an included airport (ferry, train, etc.) transfer?** This could save you money and hassle knowing you already have travel arrangements.

• **Is breakfast included?** Another great perk. If you eat enough in the morning you may be able to get away with only a small snack for lunch.

• **What is the proximity to shopping, transit, and convenience stores?** Unless you are planning on renting a vehicle or love walking for hours, choosing a cheaper accommodation further out will cost you more in the long run if you are having to pay for private transportation back and forth.

Filtering Booking Sites

When I choose accommodations I would filter first by cost (I wanted to find the cheapest accommodation that I could be comfortable with), then I would filter out customer review ranks below 6 or 7 out of 10. For me, this meant there was good value, the accommodations would be clean, and the place fairly maintained. I would then sort by map view, looking for something as close to the downtown centre as possible. In larger cites, such as Tokyo and Hong Kong, the downtown centre wasn't essential since their transit systems are so well organized that I would try to find something close to any subway station. By only booking a night or two at my first accommodation in those cities, it would also give me the opportunity to switch hotels partway through my stay and experience a different part of the city entirely.

Occasionally Splurge

Although I did my best to choose the cheapest accommodations, outside of bunkbeds or shared rooms, occasionally I would choose experience, even if it was a splurge. Some of the splurges included:

• Traditional ryokan in Tokyo

• Bungalow with infinity pools overlooking the jungle and rice fields in Bali

• Treehouse in Thailand

• Full-Moon Party centric hotel in Thailand

• Four-star hotel in Dubai for only slightly more than a budget hotel because I was there during Ramadan, which is low tourism.

• A forced splurge on a bungalow in Mykonos during their high tourism season of August. The only other accommodation that was available was bed in a 12-bed room at a hostel, which was not for me. But by keeping my travel plans open I was able to leave Mykonos the next day for the more reasonably priced Ios, Greece.

AirBnB and Couch Surfing

Although I didn't use AirBnB or any couch surfing websites, this is also an amazing way to find accommodations. I don't want to always say cheap, because sometimes it is worth splurging on a unique location. The positive about AirBnB is if you are choosing to rent a room or a bed, you also have the opportunity to meet with the local host and receive recommendations about interesting hotspots in the neighbourhood. You have the opportunity to fully immerse yourself in a location and for at least a few nights feel like you are actually living there.

AirBnB is an excellent option if you are planning on staying at any location for more than a couple of nights, right up to a few months. You have the opportunity to have all the amenities of being at home, but at someone else's home. I knew a woman that spent three months travelling through South Western Europe and used AirBnB for her stays of a week and beyond. She said she loved the entire experience.

Couch surfing is similar to AirBnB, but the cheapest option. You are essentially being given a couch to sleep on for free or a minimal cost.

With both couch surfing and AirBnB please take extra precautions to protect your safety.

Camping

Another option during the heat of the summer is to explore campgrounds and tent. The only additional cost would be of a small tent, and perhaps a mat or a thin sleeping bag. This only makes financial sense if the cost of the camping equipment and campgrounds in total is less than a few nights in a hotel. Although most people that choose to camp do so for experience over cost savings.

Be willing to part with the tent and sleeping bag once the camping experience is finished, if you decided to purchase instead of renting. You may be lucky enough to return or sell the equipment and return a portion of the costs.

The weight of the equipment will likely put you over the luggage allowance and it may not be worth paying over weight fees. The cost of shipping your newly purchased equipment back home may equal to the same price or more of what you spent to purchase the equipment to begin with.

There are some locations that have set up cots and permanent tents to explore. The ones I found were part of my tour groups, but with a little bit of research, you will likely find these prearranged campgrounds for the single traveler.

Reaching Out To Your Connections

For every friend and connection you have your friends and connection have the same number in their circle. This is an amazing opportunity to reach out, blast your FaceBook friends, tweet or any other way you can reach out and let people know where and when you plan on being at a certain location. People are willing to help out other people. The world is becoming a smaller place, and if you are willing to put out the ask, there will be someone willing to provide you with the answer. There are plenty of people that are willing to open their door to a foreign traveler excited to see their home town. Similar to the AirBnB experience, you will likely have someone willing to show you around or at least give you tips on the hot spots. You may even be lucky enough to stay for free. You never know until you ask.

Booking With Points

If you have them, use them. If you are lucky enough to have build up your credit card points enough to redeem for a flight or hotel, definitely are advantage of this. Depending on your credit card provider and the conditions they put around booking with points this could be either a benefit, or not worth the trouble.

Some credit cards limit which travel days are available, which airlines qualify, and may require a certain timeframe in advance. Other credit cards do not have any conditions and it is as seamless as booking any other flight.

It is entirely up to you how you decide to use your points. Make sure you are guaranteed to leave on the day you chose, otherwise change flight fees may not be worth the savings by using points. They may also charge the same amount of points for a roundtrip ticket as a one-way, so be sure you are maximizing your points.

In my case I saved all my points, and at the end of the trip I was able to book another vacation from Australia to Canada, well after the round the world trip was complete.

Little Luxuries

Traveling on a budget can be difficult, especially when it is over an extended period of time. Do not feel guilty if the after a while the moving every few days, eating street food, or in my case, missing getting dressed up, starts to get to you. The benefits of being a world traveler while you are financially better off than your 20-something year old counterparts is you do have the luxury of treating yourself out every now and then.

Airport Lounges

When I was working through my credit cards, one of the card features was airport lounge access passes. This by itself is a treat. Some airport lounges will do not require you to be a member and you may be able to buy a pass upon arrival, especially if you have a layover of several hours. The facilities are always beautiful, there are plenty of comfy chairs, outlets, free WiFi, and yes, free food and alcoholic beverages. This by itself may be enough to push you into getting into the airport lounges.

For me, this was a massive benefit while I was waiting for my flight to Istanbul from Dubai.

Alcohol in Dubai is scarce, unless you are at a 5-star hotel, and it is almost completely unlikely at any general public location. However in the airport lounge, the wine was non-stop and free.

Some of the larger airport lounges will have access to showers, massage therapist (for an additional cost), and TV screening areas.

Upgraded Hotels

If you happen to be traveling to any regions during their low season, you can often get a great deal on four and five-star hotels. Budget hotels don't often discount that significantly during the low-season, but the premium hotels do. You will be better able to tell if it is a low season if you are booking through a site such as booking.com and it indicates the availability of rooms are quite high. It will have a meter on the page, and usually anything below 30% could give you a great opportunity for an upgraded hotel for a more reasonable price. You may not be able to get a room for the same price as the budget hotel, but after traveling for months, a high-end mattress may be worth the extra dollars.

Alcohol

It is still possible to stay within budget and treat yourself out. Many places will offer happy hour, or reduced alcohol prices, at select times in the late afternoon. This may or may not also include reduced food prices as well. Restaurants are generally not busy during these hours and to help entice people to come, they will offer these discounts. This is the ideal time for the traveler who does't have a specific place to be. If you are lucky enough you may be able to be satisfied with a late lunch/ early dinner for the evening.

Generally if you enjoy drinking alcohol doing so in the lunch hour would be better for you, budget-wise, over saving your alcoholic drink for the evening. Restaurants will sometimes offer lunchtime drink specials, but even if they don't, restaurants usually function more efficiently during the afternoon. Since many diners are looking to get back to their office, you could be in and out within an hour. This doesn't give you enough time to finish your drink and have a second, or third one before the meal arrives. However at dinner, the intention is they want diners to linger and it can be easier to drink more alcohol while waiting for the meal to be complete.

You are also more likely to drink less in the afternoon than at dinner because being day-drunk can be a waste, where there are still more activities to see and do.

Entertainment

You now have the luxury of time. Embrace this opportunity! Theatre performances will often have reduced rates on their ticket prices for matinee, or afternoon shows. You could go to the box office the day of, or the day before, the performance to find out if this is the case. Be sure to also ask if there is a further reduction if you buy your ticket an hour before the show, even for evening performances. You may be able to see a world class show for a fraction of the price.

Google search or ask the front desk of your hotel about any festivals or events that are going on during the length of your stay. You may be in for a treat for some free street performances.

Laundry Service

You will never be happier than when you pay to have laundry taken care of by a professional.

There are plenty of places you can find laundry service, including hotel front desks. However, it is sometimes cheaper to find a local store. Hotels will typically charge by item whereas the local shops will charge by weight. This is one luxury that is very well worth it.

Massages, Spas and Salons

In many Asian countries it is possible to find many massage places, foot spas, kissing fish spas, and other unique local specialties. It may seem like an unnecessary expense, but the relaxation you will feel will be well worth it. You will have no idea how sore your muscles have been until you have someone kneading the tightness out of them.

Nail and hair salons are also a great way of treating yourself to some luxury time. Although there is nothing more entertaining than trying to describe what you would like done with your hair when you are facing language barriers. It is best to be open-minded and go with the flow. It is just hair.

Say Yes

There will be more opportunities to treat yourself out to a variety of experiences, including hot air balloons, champagne sunrises on the Serengeti, evening boat cruises, and anything else that may come up. This is not the time to limit yourself. Many of these locations you may never see again in your lifetime, but the experience you had while you were there will be forever stamped in your memory.

Currency and Money Exchange

Before getting on that first plane, ensure you inform your bank(s) and credit card(s) that you are taking a significant trip around the world. They will likely have to put notes on your accounts to allow you to transact at various places. The last thing you want is to be in a foreign country where English may not be widely spoken and have no access to cash. Ensure you have access to online banking, to keep track of your transactions and balances, and your PIN is set to no more than four-digits. Many ATMs do not accept more than four digits.

Fees

Talk to your bank and try to negotiate a waived or lowered international ATM withdraw fee. I completely overlooked this and my bank charged me $5 per withdrawal, no matter the amount. To overcome this I would withdraw the maximum allowable either by my bank (which was set to C$500 per day) or the maximum allowable by the ATM, which in countries of low value currency was often the case. However at

$5 per transaction, over 6 months, this lead to several hundred dollars just in withdrawal fees.

The $5 fee was only the case for my debit card. In the rare occasion I had to withdraw money from my credit card a different fee was applied and the interest on cash withdraws were quite high. In those cases, my credit card would charge a fee based on a percentage of the amount withdrawn on top of the higher cash advance fee. Be aware of your best opportunities to access money.

In businesses where credit cards fees weren't applied in addition to the total, I would often use my credit card. This is most likely in higher end restaurants and almost all hotels. The exchange rate on the credit cards were reasonable and it gave me the opportunity to collect more points on my cards.

International ATMs

For the most part withdrawing cash from ATMs was relatively easy. There were only a couple of countries I had difficulty withdrawing funds, India being one of them. Most banks run on the PLUS, Cirrus or Maestro networks. Almost all of my cards run off the PLUS network, and there were only a few select ATMs where I was able to find a Cirrus network.

Check the back of your cards to see which networks each card uses. Try to have cards from at least two of the networks. International ATMs will have the logo of the network that they use, and if your card has the same logo on the back you shouldn't have any difficulty withdrawing cash.

Breaking Bills

As said before, because of the fees my bank charged per withdraw, I would ask for the maximum allowable by either my bank or the ATM. Unfortunately when withdrawing large amounts the ATM will typically give the amount in large bills, which can be very challenging when buying items, or worse, when negotiating with vendors, and *hopefully* they can break the bill, which may not always be the case in hopes to have you leave the remaining amount with them.

After withdrawing the funds, enter a bank and have them break the large bills into as many small bills as possible. Try to do this immediately following the ATM withdrawal as sometimes the teller will ask to see the ATM withdraw record to prove the currency you is not counterfeit. I would rather be walking around with more common currency sizes than the same amount of money in bills that were difficult to break. In the event I was unable to find a bank open, often large retail stores, global fast food chains, or the hotel you are staying at will likely be able to break the bills. Occasionally I would be able to break the bill at a high-end hotel, but often they require you to be a guest at the hotel for them in order to be willing to break the bills.

Cash vs Charge

In the developed countries to use credit card for all transactions. However because of the I used cash for most of my transactions. I would use a credit card when booking flights and hotels (and sometimes paying). Countries that deal primarily in cash may offer cash payment discounts, so it is worth asking when you check in. Please see the accommodations section for more information about booking and staying.

Spare Cash

As your time in a country comes to an end ensure you use up all your smaller bills and coins.

Once you leave a country, coins are completely useless, unless you like to keep them as souvenirs. Take the remainder of your cash and immediately exchange it at the currency exchange kiosk at the airport. The exchange rate won't be as favourable as it would be at a bank, but hopefully there isn't a lot of cash to exchange. If there is, perhaps exchange at a bank or currency exchange before going to the airport. However by doing it at the airport, you have the opportunity to buy any last minute items, meals or anything else you may want before boarding the plane. It is also ideal to have your next destination's local currency upon before arriving at the destination country. If you can't exchange the remaining money before departing, do it as soon as your land. Depending on the countries you are traveling to, it is more common for the airport kiosk to exchange different currencies than it is for a remote currency exchange to be able to exchange certain bills.

I would rather walk into the airport with no cash in my pockets and the ability to withdraw enough cash immediately upon arriving at the new country than to play the system and wait for the best opportunity to exchange. It is always better to run out of cash by the time you get to the airport because it is almost guaranteed to find restaurants and stores that can transact with credit card instead of having to withdraw more from an ATM.

Paying For Visas and Departure Taxes

Do make sure in the event you are arriving at a country where a visa needs to be purchased on arrival, or there is a departure tax, you do keep enough cash for that. Many countries insist that those taxes/fees are paid in cash. This is also where your emergency cash in currencies such as US Dollars and/or Euro comes in handy. Although sometimes you may be able to pay via credit card, there are times when the credit card terminals are down. If cards are accepted you may be charged an additional surcharge for card transactions or there may be one counter that takes card and several others open for cash.

Carrying Multiple Currencies

Do your best to always carry a couple of different currencies. The local is typically best, however some countries rely heavily on American currency. Places like Cambodia use American dollars

often, and have ATMs that withdraw in US Dollars. The ATM will withdraw in $20s, but most items will be $1 or $2 and it is incredibly difficult to have a $20 broken. If possible, before leaving for your trip, try to acquire a lot of small American bills. They are always great in a pinch for tipping or if you are almost completely out of cash, almost every country will accept US Dollars.

The second most common is the Euro, which can be exchanged often. Places like Turkey will have ATMs that will allow you to withdraw funds in 3 different currencies: US Dollars, Euro and Turkish Lira.

Exercise and Staying Fit

One of the things I worried about the most was how I was going to stay in shape while traveling. Without a standard schedule it was going to be difficult to fit in gym sessions and yoga classes.

However, I quickly realized I did a lot of walking while traveling. Over three times the amount than I was doing at home. I was walking to transit stations, walking around streets finding my hotel, walking around entire neighbourhoods getting a sense of my surroundings.

Then there was the weight of my bag when I was traveling between hotel locations. With 18kg-23kg on my back at any given time, this was pretty much a weight-training workout on its own.

I downloaded a couple of free apps for 5 minute workouts and yoga sessions, but I found simplicity was key. About three or four times a week I would do squats, pushups, crunches and tricep dips. In many Asian cities, particularly in China, there are adult playgrounds that take the place of gyms. When I would pass one by I would play on some of the equipment, including trying to see my improvements for chin-ups and inverted crunches.

If that is not enough for you, you can always find drop-in passes for gym facilities. When I was in Indonesia I attended a couple of outdoor yoga classes.

Beyond that there will be plenty of hiking, bicycle rentals, swimming, surfing and other activities.

Eating and Drinking

The food and drinks you are about to discover are simply amazing! Whenever possible, do your best to eat and drink from the tiny local spots. You will be served the best soup you've ever had by a child that looks too young to even know how to carry a bowl without dropping it. The best meat you will ever eat will be served from skewers from a street side BBQ. And there will be countless dishes that you have absolutely no idea what they even are. I urge you to explore and explore often. Ask the locals what it is (sometimes after trying it first), how to eat it, and for more.

If you find your stomach gets sensitive around certain local cuisines, this can sometimes be relieved by eating only vegetarian. I have heard of several people being fine when eating in India if they stay away from meat.

There will be certain customs when it comes to eating and drinking. Pay attention to those around you, and when in doubt, ask. Even beyond language, someone will usually be able to show you the correct way to eat with certain utensils.

There will be lots of local drinks to try as well. Local beers, wine, and whatever the local speciality is.

Experience lots. Try everything, even if it looks completely disgusting, like skewered scorpion, or fried crickets. In the end you will have stories more amazing than anything you could imagine.

Making Friends

One of the best parts about traveling alone is the opportunity to meet so many people. There is something about the lone traveler that makes people curious, and you more approachable.

Although people will approach you when you are traveling with someone, it happens far more frequently when you are sitting on your own.

The easiest way to meet new people is joining tour groups. There will be several people on the tour that are also solo travellers, and it is quick to get to know each other. With the length of time and proximity that you are spending with each other, it is easy to get to know each other. Some of my good friends to this day are people that I spent two weeks with on a vacation tour.

Hostels are also another great place to meet fellow travellers. Even if you chose not to stay at the hostel, many of them have restaurants, bars and welcome others into their facilities. With hostels you know everyone is also a traveler and therefore they are usually quite welcoming.

Besides that, the other option is to walk up to people and be friendly. Very few people can resist the power of the accent. You could start by introducing yourself, saying where you are from, and what countries, cities, and other places you are going to next. By asking people for advice and their opinion about places, conversations start very easily.

Many people I have met avoid traveling alone because they are afraid of not meeting people. This fear is so far off from the reality. I was able to meet locals, workers, traveler, ex-patriots, and a variety of people. Everyone with a unique story and interesting circumstance how they ended up where they were. And almost everyone I met was just as interested in my story as I was in theirs. To this day I enjoy traveling alone because of all the things I will learn about myself, the world, and of others.

Buying Items

There will be plenty of markets and opportunities to buy items. In many poorer Asian countries, such as Vietnam, Cambodia and India, there will be plenty of opportunities to purchase clothing or have pieces custom made. Many of the clothing items are coming directly from the factories and will have the company labels on their items. You will find dresses, jeans, wallets, purses, and everything else you could imagine. Whether these items were legally removed from the factories is up for you to decide. However, the deals for these items are fantastic, and this will be a great opportunity to refresh your clothing items that have been worn for too long.

If you didn't purchase a silk sleeping bed liner before leaving for your trip, places such as Vietnam, where silk is incredibly cheap, is a great place to now have one made. As well as custom suits, shirts, and other fitted outfits. Ensure you have the tailor give the clothing items a little sick since you are likely at your lowest weight from all the daily walking.

Knock-Offs and Fakes

In many places you will encounter fake items. Commonly you will see watches, wallets, purses, and pens, but there are also iPods, Beats Headphones, and cellphones, just to list a few. To find these locations it will be as common as a search engine look up. Places such as Shanghai will have entire malls dedicated to fake items, which are actually located in the back rooms of the exterior stores, whereas Kuala Lumpur will have a street market district. Many countries make it illegal to buy and ship fake items, so use your discretion.

There are good fake items and poorly constructed fake items. Do your best to understand what you are purchasing and do not pay more than you are comfortable with. Some vendors will ask for prices that are comparable to the real item prices. Do not feel bad if you refuse to pay top dollar for an item and the vendor kicks you out of their "store", it just means there are tourists paying the unreasonably high prices.

Getting Local Help

In some cases when purchasing items the vendor refuses to reduce the price. I like to call this the "tourist discount".

If you are part of a tour group, feel free to ask the tour guide to negotiate on your behalf. With local language and culture he or she may be able to get you a much better discount.

The other option, if you are a trusting person, is to ask a local to purchase the item for you. You will likely have to tip the person that is making the purchase for you as a "thank you" for going out of their way. But even with the purchase price and the tip this may be a much cheaper option.

Souvenirs

Over time you will likely be collecting a variety of souvenirs, and you don't want them weighing down your bag for too long. The best way of dealing with this is to mail them back home to yourself, or a family member for your return. It is fairly easy to find post offices around and it will take a few days to a couple of weeks to get the items back to yourself.

Safety Tips

A vast majority of the places you will visit and the people you will meet are incredibly friendly and gracious. You will be overwhelmed with the amount of love and kindness extended by perfect strangers and will quickly realize that smiles surpass all language barriers. However, here are a few extra tips to ensure you, and your belongings, stay safe wherever you travel. Be careful that you do not become arrogant as you continue to travel. There are two types of people that are often robbed, those that are oblivious, and those that are over confident.

Carry a Dummy Wallet

Consider the dummy wallet as a version of life insurance. Do not leave anywhere without it.

A dummy wallet is a fake wallet that will have some cash in it. Usually US$100 is more than enough. Stuff it with a few receipts and fake cards, like old hotel keys, a library card and any card that looks like a fake credit card. It should feel thick and real enough that it seems like your actual wallet.

Place it in your day bag and carry it with you at all times. Put it in a pocket that is easily accessible by both yourself and pickpockets. In the event, you are pickpocketed the thief will find the wallet first and won't bother trying to slice your bag or some other riskier action.

If you are put in a more compromising position, most people would rather have money than to harm. If you are in a dangerous situation, such as being mugged, pull the wallet out quickly and throw it in the opposite direction that you run. The thief will likely go after the money and you will save yourself. Thankfully, you will also still have the remainder of your money, your passport, and all credit cards.

However, please use your instincts and do not try to be a hero. When I was traveling there was a story about a British woman who was hospitalized because she refused to give up her bag when she was at knifepoint. Stories like this are incredibly rare, but it is a powerful warning to all travellers that nothing in this world is more important than your safety.

Split Up Cards and Money

On top of your Dummy Wallet you will also carry two more wallets. Each wallet will have a portion of your money and credit cards split up. They will be carried and kept separately. In the event your hotel room is raided or you are robbed while out, you will still have access to money and credit. As long as you have access to money you are well taken care of.

When traveling with all your items keep one wallet in your money belt with your passport and keep the second in your day bag or a zipped pocket that never leaves you. However, after you drop off your backpack at the hotel or hostel, lock your passport and one of the wallets up in the safe, and explore and shop with the second.

Use A Money Belt But Don't Wear It

Your money belt should only be worn only when your hostel or hotel does not have a safe for you to keep your passport, additional credit cards, and cash, or if you are commuting between locations. Many people wear their money belts constantly, keep all their items in there, and every time they make a purchase, lift their shirt, and unintentionally expose everything they are carrying. At this point, they become a target for thieves as someone has seen how much they are carrying. Avoid this by doing a little preplanning before leaving your room for the day. Decide how much you will likely spend, keep that amount in a zipped up trouser pocket or zipped up pocket inside your day bag.

If you fold your money always have small bills on the outside and larger bills inside to make it look like you are carrying less money than you are. Carry one credit and/or debit card in the event you want to make a bigger purchase or need to make a cash withdrawal.

Try to always have plenty of small bills so you are not pulling out large denominations. You can always walk into any bank and ask to break up your large bills for smaller ones.

In the event, you are wearing a money belt and need to access it, do it with discretion. Access it when you are in the privacy of a toilet stall.

Maintain Your Personal Space

Do your best to always be aware of your personal space. In crowded environments, such as trains, it is easy for pick pockets to surround you and steal your wallet or other personal items without you even being aware that it is happened. If the pick pockets is daring, they will go as far as slicing your bag strap right from your body. If you wear your day bag in front of your body, you will be able to catch it in the event it is sliced.

For men, there may be times, especially in places such as Thailand where there are "lady-boys" who will surround you and start grabbing at your body. They will be flirtatious and may grab at your genitals. This will be a very quick moment, and with all the hands on your body they will have found your wallet and will have taken it before you even know what happens.

Don't Carry Weapons

Occasionally someone asks if they would be better to carry a knife. Although many people will have strong opinions I am a believer in not carrying one. I have never used a knife in any selfdefense capacity, and a "fight or flight" situation would be the worst time to try. Secondly, I don't want to have it turned against me in the event the attacker was stronger than me.

Returning to the dummy wallet point, most people want money and will run once they have that.

Bag Protectors

There are some products on the market that look like wire shells for your bag. They lock up and promise to be resistant to slicing. I saw a few travellers with these shells on their bag.

Personally I was not a fan of the wire, not because they didn't look safe, they certainly did, but because of the attention a shell creates when walking around. With the wire locked around a bag, it appear there is something valuable in the bag, and if it is left anywhere, such as checking it into an airport, leaving it on the baggage area of a ferry, and so on, the bag is more likely to go "missing" than it is to have the wire sliced. In the end that is a personal choice if you decide to splurge on a protective casing.

Consistently Keep in Touch with Home

People are going to want to know what you are doing and all the wonderful things that you are seeing. Whether that is keeping people up to date with your travels in a daily blog, updating your Instagram or Skyping your mom, do it and do it regularly, at least daily. There will be times when internet will be patchy when you are traveling through rural India or you are doing a 3-day volcano climb, but let people know this and get in contact again once you are back in reception zone. The last thing you want is to have a news story break out about a riot in a country or city that you happen to be traveling through and everyone is worried that you are in danger.

When in Doubt, Join a Tour

When I traveled solo I was determined to see India, despite the stories I heard about what it was like to travel as a solo woman, and Egypt, despite the civil unrest that was being portrayed on the news. Unfortunately being so far away from these locations there is a lot of fear-mongering in the news and individual stories make some of these places seem unsafe.

If you are still interested in visiting areas that leave you feeling uncertain thankfully many countries have professional tour operators that will ensure you are traveling safely. I chose G Adventures for India, Egypt and Jordan, a decision I am pleased to have taken. It gave me the opportunity to still experience local culture, meet new people and not miss a beat in my excursion.

Enrol With Your Embassy

Many countries will have a travel advisory and notification on your national government web page. It is best practice to always enrol with your government with your passport number and the dates that you are expected to be in each country. In the event a natural disaster or some other unforeseen event occurs in the locations you are traveling through, the government will search you out and will do their best to quickly evacuate you to a safe location.

Follow Your Gut

If it doesn't feel right, don't do it. Parties on the other side of an island, hiring a bungee jump company that doesn't give you a sense of safety, or walking through an area that doesn't give you a sense of security, and your instincts are saying to take a tuk-tuk, always go with what feels right. There's something about your gut knowing what is best in that moment. You will never look back on your life and say, "I wish I went to one more beach party" but you may regret a decision that didn't feel right in the first place.

Street Children and Beggars

Every country you visit, there will be plenty of beggars and street children. As a tourist you will sometimes think you look like a giant dollar side walking down the street but don't let this deter your experience.

Children Selling Items

There will be plenty of street children selling items in various locations. There are split opinions on whether it is "right" to buy and support the children (and arguably their families) in these situations. If the children are selling items during the day, they are obviously not attending school. Some of the children will say they are trying to make money in order to school, but it becomes a catch-22. If the child was to make enough money selling items or begging in order to afford to go to school, they likely never will, because they are bringing in too much income to make it justifiable to use that time for school. One of the ways I would get around this moral dilemma is I would chat with the children about their education during hours I believed they should be in school to test how much they are learning, if anything. I would be willing to purchase items in the evening when they likely would not be attending school. This would teach the children that they could attend both school and make an income selling items.

Begging Scams

Children ask you for coins in your home currency or other currencies. They will tell you that they like to collect them. This may be the case, but more likely they collect the coins and then immediately find another tourist who will be able to exchange the coins for bills, which then are exchanged for local currency. It's a long begging form, but it pays off because it is almost completely unsuspecting.

There was one scam when I was in Cambodia where a child, carrying a toddler asked me to buy him and his little brother milk. When he dragged me into the store, the child changed his mind and asked me to buy an $18 tin of formula, and then followed up saying he could buy two tins for $30. The ask then changed from buying the tins to just giving money. The child got very aggressive when I insisted "no", grabbed me, and thankfully did not steal anything.

Local "Friends"

In some locations locals will approach you and ask you out for dinner, drinks, or other "dates".

They may say they are trying to learn English, or they are "interested" in dating. If you do decide to meet with them, be fully aware to the progression of the evening. The locals will leave close to the end of the evening of drinks and food, and never return. The server will return with the bill for the entire meal, and perhaps a bit more, if the locals ordered take-away meals in addition.

Wearing Makeup and Going Out

Since you will be carrying a limited number of items in your backpack you likely won't have your regular items you wear for going out. This is a great experience of simplicity.

Makeup

With limited space in your backpack you obviously won't be taking all the makeup you would typically wear on your average day. For some women this could be difficult to adjust to and will insist it is too important and take it with them anyway. However, for the amount of time you will be traveling why not go without?

I went with only the basics; eyeliner, mascara and a BB Cream. I was surprised by the number of people that still found me incredibly attractive with only bare essentials. And I only wore it if I was planning on going out for a night.

I never wore makeup on a standard day. I felt I didn't need to. I was sightseeing. I was pushing myself out of my comfort zone on many days, and going almost six months without makeup was something else I never tried before.

Hair

Also because there is such limited space any type of hair products or styling devices will likely be left behind. Become an expert in braids, top knots, or use the natural beach wave that will come after a day of water sports.

Shoes

If your standard sandals are gold or black they are perfect to wear out to many places. I did pack a pair of ultra flat sandals for going out but I ended up throwing them out within a couple of months. They were stuffed and tossed around so much in my bag, and although they withstood some wet and rainy environments a couple of times, they were destroyed faster than I expected. For the handful of times I wore them it wasn't worth replacing them.

Purse

I bought a waterproof black cosmetic bag, which during my travels contained toiletries, but it was nice enough to use as a clutch when I was going out. It was large enough that my camera could fit in, but small enough to easily fit under my shoulder.

The only other bag I carried was my day bag, which I did use if I was planning on being out for a longer period of time than a simple evening. With the day bag I would have enough room to carry my sunglasses and my iPad, if I was searching for a location, or needed language skills. However, today I would purchase a cell phone, that could replace the few things I needed the iPad for during an evening out.

Dresses

I wore a lot of dresses while I was traveling because they were easy, so I always had something to wear. If you are struggling deciding on a dress, my personal favorite was a coral 5-way dress.

It was bright enough that it was fashionable, and the 5-way allowed me to tie it in such a way that it could look like a halter, strapless, or in a way that covered my shoulders for a completely different look.

Jewelry

I would wear a fashionable necklace and earrings to help glamourize my outfit. Since I wasn't purchasing many souvenirs, jewelry was my primary souvenir of choice. Jewelry pieces were cheap enough that if they ever were stolen, I wouldn't be upset, plus they looked fashionable without looking real, which you do not want to draw too much attention to yourself, especially in poorer countries.

Dressing Up For Men

Men can get away with a lot less when going out. Sandals are completely appropriate to wear to many places. Ensure you have a decent pair of traveling pants, which you will wear typically for colder days, but could pass in a nice venue. A collared golf shirt, or some other dry-wick fabric that looks nice would be sufficient.

Wedding Ring

I bought a small band in a market that I wore on my left hand even though not all cultures wear wedding bands, or wear them on their left hand.

Traveling alone as a female, I felt wearing the band gave me a quick escape from conversations that started to get uncomfortable. Especially in some Asian countries, they are incredibly curious about females traveling alone and either have numerous questions, or want to set you up and marry you off. By telling people that I am married, and my husband is here for business and I am doing some sightseeing while he is in meetings very quickly put an end to many conversations.

I didn't lie all the time. I read my audience and choose to be truthful or use my story. Often times, though, it was a lot easier when people assumed I was a married woman.

Etiquette

Every culture has it's little nuances. When in doubt, ask a local what is okay. People are usually excited that you asked and they are happy to explain their culture to you.

Although this isn't a comprehensive list, here are a few things I learned on my travels. You can read travel blogs to learn more, or better yet, experience it first hand. This is by no means an expert list and may not be completely accurate.

When it came to eating I would always observe a few people and their etiquette before picking up utensils.

General Etiquette
• Always ask before taking anyone's picture. Even with language barriers, people will understand if you show them your camera.
• Please and Thank You go so incredibly far. Same with language, if you do not know how to say it, ask, or a simple, modest smile, and bow will usually suffice.
• If you do not know, ask. Better to ask than to assume. And just because you see locals doing it, it does not mean you are privileged to enter a building, sit on a pew, or are dressed appropriately. Tourism is for everyone,

and it would be terrible for a couple of rude tourists to ruin the perception locals have on all of us.

Australia

• ALWAYS take the time for small talk: "How was your day?" "What are you up to later?"
Australians see anything less as being rude

• If someone in the group says they are going to be bar to order themselves a drink, and you are in need of one, ask for one. Australians will not offer to get a drink, they are expecting an ask. I was told by a local that it is considered a sign of gratitude. You would only ask if you would be willing to return the favor if it was asked of you. If you choose to wait until the person returns, and then you get your own drink you risk insulting your company.

• If there is something that you would like, or something is not to your liking, ask politely for an adjustment. Australians are very accommodating people and they will always respond positively to a request. They struggle heavily with complaints and often don't know if the person is complaining to complain or if they are complaining because they want something else.

• Questions are not provided with inflections. Conversations require a lot of participation.
Always assume every statement is a question and immediately agree (or disagree)

• They wait to be invited into conversations. If you are interested in talking to someone you can outright ask them their opinion or if they would like to join.

Cambodia

• Khmer food is eaten with a fork and a spoon. Use the fork to portion the main dish onto the rice. You then eat with the spoon. Do not pour the entire main dish on the rice. Small portions at a time.

• Before taking a sip of your drink, you are to clink glasses, or "cheers" everyone around you. If you are bing "cheered" you do not have to drink at the same time. This can be a tough adjustment for those of us that are accustom to drinking after every glass clink.

China

• Many queues are on a "first-come-first-serve" basis. This does not mean that you are waiting in line for your turn. This does mean you have to be willing to be very assertive and push your way to the front when in a queue.

• Assertiveness will also benefit you when walking down the street, and dodging traffic. Cars and scooters are not limited to only the roads. Be fully aware of your surroundings.

Japan

• Slurping of soup is a sign that you are enjoying it. So please slurp.

• Money is not to be exchanged hand to hand. It is to be placed in the tray sitting on the counter. Change will be provided back in the same manner

• Never pour your own beverage. The person next to you will serve you your drink. You will return the favor

• NEVER tip. Do not leave remaining change. It is seen as an insult. A local explained to me that it is a sign that the service you provided was not enough and by tipping you are hoping they will do better next time

• Always queue. There are designated queue spaces for getting onboard a subway

• Smoking is highly restricted. There are designated smoking areas in the streets of Tokyo

• Always accept gifts offered and return the favor by sending one in return

• Depending on the restaurant ordering food may be done at a machine located close to the entrance, once you have placed your order then you may find a place to sit

Jordan

• Order your shisha at the beginning of the meal, before the meal. The hot stones will be refreshed throughout the meal. The server will stop refreshing them when the meal is served, and re-start them once your meal is completed. Feel free to ask for hot stones whenever the shisha becomes a little bitter.

Tanzania

• Food offered must always be tried. It is rude to refuse food without trying it first. No one cares if you are not hungry

Turkey

• As a very modest country, everything is very quietly spoken, conversations are lengthened, and dinners are an all evening affair. Take your time, and get to know your company.

• There isn't a lot of acceptance for "hooting" and "hollering". The people are a lot of fun, but boisterousness is not seen as an appealing quality.

Vietnam

• People will lead you either with their arm hooked into yours or by hand. You need to be okay with physical touch by strangers

• Full body massages include the *full*-body. As a woman if you will be uncomfortable having your breasts touched, let the massage therapist know this beforehand.

• Pho is eaten by making a sauce base for the meat. You then use your chopsticks to pull the meat out, dip it in the sauce, and then proceed to the eat the rest of the soup as you would. Do not over complicate the tastes by pouring sauce into the soup directly.

Homesickness

Homesickness is a funny thing. You will enjoy every moment of your trip, and suddenly you will be hit with a moment of sadness. You will miss certain things about being home. It will always be something that you never expected to miss either.

By the end of my trip I really missed simple things; new music, movies, and hanging out with friends, were some of the things I missed the most.

Everyone will have something that will trigger homesickness at some point. The best way to get over it is to continue to go out. There is so much to look forward to.

Book a call date with your family and friends, which can often be difficult because it never fails that homesickness hits when it's the middle of the night back at home.

Go out and meet people. If you're not staying at a hostel, find the closest hostel bar. Likely everyone there has been in a similar position.

Sit at the bar and chat up the bartender.

If the homesickness gets really bad know that you are literally one or two flights away from getting home. I promise you the homesickness will pass before you actually book that flight.

Keeping Track of Your Journey

Everyone is going to want to know every part of your journey. People are going to want to live vicariously through your adventure. When you return the questions are going to be non-stop. It is up to you if you would like to keep your journey private and personal, or if you would like to share it with just your group of friends or the world.

I highly recommend keeping track of your journey while you are on it. You will forget little details and simple things about every day. The days will feel long and mellow, but the weeks and months will fly by instantly. Make it a habit to keep track of something everyday. Many people I met tried to journal write, but easily the days took over and they were playing "catchup" on entries from a week before. I chose to write a blog on a free, travel constructed site. I chose this method because it was easy, it allowed me to download my photos instantly, it notified my network of new entries and I had the option to purchase a hardcover book with all my entries and photos inside it.

Whatever method you choose to use to keep track of your journey ask yourself why that method? And why is this so important? What do you hope to have once your journey is done?

By understanding the importance of why you are doing what you are doing you will be better situated to continue to do it daily.

Cameras

Many new cameras have WiFi which allows you to download your photos instantly. This means during a long bus journey or while waiting in the airport for your next flight you can start to download your photos onto your iPad, or whatever device you decide to bring with you. This ensures you will never lose more than a day or two of photos if the worst was to happen.

Many new cell phones have amazing cameras on them, and I was impressed with their photo taking capabilities. If you are not a person that knows how to use an SLR camera, there is absolutely nothing wrong with using your phone. Plus you can update your social media much more easily.

A word of caution about SLR cameras: unless you are a professional photographer you may want to opt for something smaller. I am not a professional photographer, but I did want to take high quality photos. I asked for the best quality camera that could fit in my pocket. I wanted something better than a point-and-shoot, but not the bulkiness of an SLR. SLRs are often heavy and with the different accessories you are bringing they can be cumbersome. Plus, you want to look like an ex-pat in as many places as possible. It is hard to negotiate when you are carrying a small bag of camera equipment. In poorer countries this can also be a flag and you will look like a muggers best bet. There are too many items that they are willing to go after. If you choose to go with an SLR know what you are preparing yourself for.

Ideas on recording

If you are wanting to record your journey but are not one for writing, here's a couple of ideas:

• Write a sentence a day. That's it. One sentence that captures the highlight for that day

• Take one-second of video everyday. Put it together in a video at the end. It will capture amazing things and the whirl-wind that your trip was

• Create a theme video. In each city you are in take video of you dancing (or planking or I knew one guy who did "whaling", a video of him leaping out from behind various walls, buildings or other unexpected places) with locals, tour groups or anything else you can think of.

• Blog on a specific topic. If you love food, use every opportunity to only explore the food items you found and ate. This also works for transportation, nightlife, hotels, beaches, or anything else you can think of.

• Use social media for recording your location and the things you do. Instagram, Periscope and Foursquare are great apps for recording your location and what you are doing.

Recording your journey is supposed to be fun, and not a make work project. Ideally think about how committed you are to record, and even the best intentions can easily fall on the wayside when the excitement and exhaustion of a day sets in. Know the minimum you can commit to and stick with that. If you succeed and create more, great. If not, you will be happy you were able to stick to your minimum commitment, which over the course of several months is a huge achievement.

Coming Home

Even if you've been blogging or updating your Facebook every day you are away the moment anyone sees you the first thing you are asked is "what was your favorite place?" How do you answer such a question? You've more than likely seen amazing things, every culture is different, the same ocean looks different from Japan to Vietnam to Australia to Los Angeles. It is difficult to describe how the air smelled in Sydney and how spicy street samosas were in Delhi and the sound of applause from the entire island of Santorini when the sun sets. Yet after numerous flights, trains, buses, and motorcycle taxis the question is "what was your favorite place?"

I wish there was an easy answer and you have a couple of options. You could mention a few of the highlights but even that won't do your trip justice. Eventually you'll just have a single word answer: Vietnam (or whatever country you choose). It's not to simplify your experience. You will always have that. It just makes it easier because the majority of the people in the world haven't come close to experiencing what you just did. In a single trip you have likely seen more of the world than more people will see in their lifetime.

I've heard of people setting up photo nights as they scroll through the photos of all the places they've seen, but remember to even keep this limited. Attention spans are short and you won't be able to hold anyone's attention for longer than an hour or so. Maybe two, if it's your mom.

Going Back to Work

If you were lucky enough to take a sabbatical from your work, there will be no bigger relief than finally having a routine again. You will have a specific time to wake up everyday, you will have a purpose and feel like you are providing a contribution again. You are more than likely going to be excited to go back.

If you were like me, and had to quit your job in order to travel, there is the long search of finding a new role. During your travels, you may have realized you were meant for something else in this world. You will now have the opportunity to pursue this new passion. You will be asked a lot of questions about your resumé gap. Some interviewers are genuinely interested in knowing about your trip. They will want to know what you learned about yourself and others.

Occasionally there will be a recruiter that will challenge you on taking off. This seems completely absurd to them, know that this is likely not the role or company that you would want to work for. Anyone that can't see leaving to travel and learn so much about people and culture would never understand any organizational changes you would be willing to bring or new ways of completing old tasks. The positive changes you could implement because of your new knowledge would never resonate with that organization.

It could take as little as a few weeks to several months to find a new job. Be prepared for that. I financially budgeted quite well when I was on my trip, even though I went 10% over. However, I forgot to budget for the time that I was without work and looking for a job. Thankfully I had my family's support and for the months that I was back and searching I had them to help me out.

In order to budget for this time of job hunting take any fixed expenses: housing, vehicle, personal care, and going out. Assume the time to find a position will take anywhere from six weeks to six months. The amount of time you budget for will also depend on when you are planning on returning as companies will slow down hiring during the summer breaks and December/New Year time frame.

Coming Back Into Routine

When you come home there will be plenty of things that you enjoyed doing before you left that no longer have the same appeal. For me it was TV watching and celebrity news and gossip.

Once I returned, having spent months watching minimal TV, I completely lost the appeal for it. However, being back into the old routine it was there and I found myself slowly watching more TV than I was comfortable with. It took a lot of willpower and eventually I found a comfort level, and a way of finding myself being more conscious of the TV in the background.

Many people also claim to have a sight depression or at least boredom when they return. Being away you will spend every day doing something; something amazing, something ordinary but always exploring and being a part of the local life. Returning home can be quite the opposite as you find yourself staying in. This is great for the first while, but you may quickly be searching for your next flight and feeling like you need to be on the move again. Understand this happens to every one. Do what's best for you.

Closing

Although I did my best to include every aspect of traveling as I could I know there is likely many areas that I missed out.

By no means was my "world-trip" completely comprehensive, but it was the best I could do with the time and budget I had. There are plenty of people with far more experience, who have been traveling for far longer periods of time. There are plenty of resources on the internet that will help you with any specific areas that you have questions for.

This guide is to help inspire you and let you know that a travel sabbatical is much easier than you could ever imagine. I hope this helps you get your journey started. Remember this is your journey. Do what feels right and excites you. Your memories will be carried with you forever.

Please contact me when you have embarked on your own journey. My goal is to inspire, and I am grateful you have given me the opportunity to do so.

Good luck. Stay safe. Prepare to be amazed at the wonders of the world, and the wonders the world shows you about yourself.

Printed in the United States
By Bookmasters